TEN
ACROBATS IN
AN AMAZING
LEAP OF FAITH

Yussef El Guindi

BROADWAY PLAY PUBLISHING INC
New York
www.broadwayplaypub.com
info@broadwayplaypub.com

Cover art by Drew Skwish

First edition: February 2018
I S B N: 978-0-88145-754-4

Book design: Marie Donovan
Page make-up: Adobe InDesign
Typeface: Palatino

TEN ACROBATS IN AN AMAZING LEAP OF FAITH
was commissioned by Cornerstone Theater Company.
The play received its world premiere at Silk Road
Rising in Chicago in 2005. The cast and creative
contributors were as follows:

KAMAL.. Vincent P Mahler
MONA .... Irit Levit
TAWFIQ .... Kareem Bandealy
HAMZA ....Anil Hurkadli
HUWAIDA ....Monica Lopez
MURAD .... Peter Nicholas
AZIZ ....Frank Platis
PAULINE .... Mary Ann de la Cruz
H D ....Jen Albert
KEVIN..Steven Gilpin

Director ....Stuart Carden
Set design .... Matthew Morton
Lighting design ....Kurt Ottinger
Sound design & original music ....Robert Steele
Costume design .... Aly Greaves
Stage manager ....Alexandra Herryman

CHARACTERS & SETTING

KAMAL, *father*
MONA, *mother*
HUWAIDA, *daughter*
TAWFIQ, *son*
HAMZA, *son*
AZIZ, *good friend of* MONA *and* KAMAL
MURAD, *son of* AZIZ

PAULINE, *therapist to* HUWAIDA
KEVIN, *connects with* HAMZA
H D, HUWAIDA's *dream double*

Above cast can also double for: VEILED FIGURES, PILOT'S
VOICE, CUSTOMS OFFICER, BOMB SQUAD.

Time: the present
Setting: Los Angeles

AUTHOR'S NOTE:

When the play was first produced at Silk Road Rising, there were not enough Arab American actors to be found in the Chicago area. So we cast different ethnicities to play the roles. I would encourage future productions to do the same. If Arab American actors can be found, great, if not, feel free to cast your net further afield.

THANKS

To Corey Pond and Jamil Khoury for helping me
assemble some of the material for publication.

DEDICATION

For Jamil Khoury and Malik Gillani.
Thank you for stepping in and first producing the play.

ACT ONE

Scene 1

(Possible pre-show music: sound of an oud. Beautiful, lyrical. As the play starts, this will change into occasionally painful, halting sounds. It is heard off-stage.)

(KAMAL and TAWFIQ are in the living room, which is bare of furniture. Both men are polishing the floor. KAMAL is shuffling along, a rag under his feet. TAWFIQ is pushing a mop before him. He is also either bare-footed or in socks.)

(This goes on for a few beats before TAWFIQ stops what he's doing, looks at his father, and addresses him with some resolve.)

TAWFIQ: Ba-ba.

(KAMAL doesn't seem to hear TAWFIQ and continues to clean.)

TAWFIQ: Ba-ba.

(Again, no response)

TAWFIQ: Ba-ba!

(KAMAL turns to TAWFIQ just as MONA appears at the doorway.)

KAMAL: *(Accent)* What? *(He then remembers to take his earplugs out.)* What is the matter?

MONA: *(Accent)* Who's going to speak to him, you or me?

KAMAL: What are you talking about?

(A particularly painful sound from the oud is heard.)

MONA: You're his father. He'll listen.

KAMAL: He's getting in touch with his roots.

MONA: What roots? These sounds come from a country that is not on the map.

KAMAL: He's better.

MONA: In theory. In practice, he is killing us today.

KAMAL: It takes time.

MONA: A little too long.

KAMAL: There are no shortcuts to learning a musical instrument. There is agony, and then there are the sweet sounds of someone who has not given up. Someone who continues in spite of the problems. Who refuses to rest until his passion is answered by the sounds he knows his beloved instrument possesses.

(Another particularly harsh sound from the oud.)

KAMAL: I'll go speak to him. *(Starts for the door)* He doesn't have to practice all day.

MONA: He can go to the park. Perhaps nature will inspire him.

KAMAL: *(Close to her; perhaps cups her face with his hands.)* Did I mention how beautiful you are today?

MONA: Yes, but you can tell me again.

KAMAL: You are the light on my dark nights.

MONA: Mmm.

KAMAL: You are the blue in my morning skies.

MONA: More.

KAMAL: You are the water that brings back to life my dry heart and makes it speak in little cooing sounds.

TAWFIQ: Excuse me. Would you like me to leave?

KAMAL: Why? Would you prefer to watch us argue instead?

TAWFIQ: No. But... Never mind. *(He starts mopping again.)*

KAMAL: *(To* MONA*)* It is not cool to be in love.

MONA: At our age, he has a point.

KAMAL: We'd better quarrel for the sake of our son. Any particular quarrel you would like?

MONA: You choose.

KAMAL: I'm in too good a mood, you begin.

MONA: I am afraid they will start soon enough without my help.

KAMAL: In that case let us say we quarreled and make up.

MONA: Agreed.

KAMAL: That was quick. You know, in this country, married people sometimes marry each other again. Renewing their vows they call it. When our daughter gets engaged, why not we make it a double ceremony? I feel like taking a second wife. I would like my second wife to be you.

MONA: As your first wife, I second that. For the sake of your health. You wouldn't live long enough to enjoy another woman.

KAMAL: We do it then? *(To* TAWFIQ*)* Tawfiq: you never saw us get married, did you.

MONA: He wouldn't have.

KAMAL: *(To* TAWFIQ*)* Would you like that? How often do children see their parents marrying? One good thing about this country is that old people don't have to act old if they don't want to. They can be as young as they want to be.

MONA: Go ask your son first to take a break. Then I can feel romantic again. But be kind; don't discourage him.

KAMAL: *(As he exits)* He can bring the oud with him and practice after prayers. The pigeons can be his audience for a change.

(KAMAL exits. TAWFIQ continues to mop.)

TAWFIQ: I wouldn't put him off it. It's the one thing he enjoys.

MONA: I want him to continue. He *is* getting better…. I needed to talk to you. *(Takes a breath)* Tawfiq…I would like to know what is going on.

TAWFIQ: What do you mean?

MONA: Tawfiq, please.

TAWFIQ: Can we leave it alone?

MONA: That is not possible with me, you know that.

TAWFIQ: There's nothing more to say. I've already told you how I feel. It's not a big deal.

MONA: Are you still going to tell him? …If it's not a big thing, then you don't have to tell him.

TAWFIQ: And you want me to do what? Lie?

MONA: It's not a lie if you don't say anything. Nobody asked you a question.

TAWFIQ: And when I go pray with him, what is that?

MONA: It's being a good son.

TAWFIQ: You brought me up better than that.

MONA: Then tell him next week. After the engagement. Why tell him today?

TAWFIQ: Someone needs to stop that. I mean it. She doesn't know what she's doing.

MONA: Do not concern yourself with that, it's none of your business.

TAWFIQ: It is my business when I see my sister walking into something this stupid.

MONA: Worry about your own life, it's her choice.

TAWFIQ: Oh, bull. She may think it's her choice but it's not.

MONA: What's gotten into you? —When did you become so hard? That you think you can speak to me like that? And your father: to want to tell him this? Really, what is happening? You're short tempered now. You don't sit with us. You used to laugh. What happened to my son who used to laugh?

TAWFIQ: I just don't want to pretend anymore.

MONA: Why not, it's easy. You keep it to yourself until this nonsense you are in passes.

TAWFIQ: It's not nonsense.

MONA: It's not necessary.

TAWFIQ: Didn't you both bring me up to always tell the truth?

MONA: The truth is not a knife you stab someone with. What do you achieve by telling him? Is it fasting you're fed up with?

TAWFIQ: Oh, mom, stop.

MONA: It's not the end of the world if you don't want to fast. We'll make up some excuse to your father.

TAWFIQ: It has nothing to do with that.

MONA: Is it some course you're taking in college?

TAWFIQ: *No.*

MONA: Then what? One day you're a Muslim and the next you decide everything you grew up believing is now stupid? A joke?

TAWFIQ: I didn't say that. I just said—I don't want to be a part of something that doesn't make sense to me anymore.

(At some point during the above exchange, the sound of the oud has stopped.)

MONA: Then don't. No one is forcing you to. But you don't have to tell your father; and you don't have to tell him today.

TAWFIQ: I don't want to go to prayers with him.

MONA: Okay, we'll make up some excuse.

TAWFIQ: I don't want to lie to him.

MONA: Instead you just want to twist his heart and break it.

TAWFIQ: Thinking God is a fairy tale is not a crime.

MONA: I'm not talking about you or what you believe. Believe what you want. But you don't have to drag it in here and hit us over the head with it.

TAWFIQ: What do you think you've been doing with me? With all of us? For all these years?

(For a second, it looks like MONA might slap TAWFIQ. But she doesn't.)

MONA: Is that what we've been doing? —And what you want to do helps you how?

TAWFIQ: I get to breathe…I finally get to breathe.

(KAMAL enters.)

KAMAL: I was gentle. I told him the house wasn't big enough to hold his musical ambitions. We should look into renting him a studio. *(He takes a second mop leaning against a wall.)* Are we finished here; or—shall we wait until after we return? *(Noticing the mood change in the room)* What did I miss? —What did you say to upset your mother?

MONA: Nothing. Tawfiq can't come with you and Hamza today.

KAMAL: Why not? We were going to call on 'Am Aziz afterwards.

MONA: He has a meeting with a college professor.

KAMAL: Oh? Is everything okay?

MONA: It's just about a project he's working on.

KAMAL: Why are you talking for him? *(To* TAWFIQ*)* Is everything okay?

TAWFIQ: Yes; everything's fine.

KAMAL: No problems at university?

TAWFIQ: No.

KAMAL: Then I can meet this professor. *(Calling out)* Hamza. Get ready. We're leaving now.

TAWFIQ: It's okay, we don't have to meet him today.

KAMAL: Why not. It's about time I met one of your teachers.

TAWFIQ: We can do it later.

KAMAL: If we're dropping you off, I might as well.

TAWFIQ: It's not like high-school, you don't have to.

KAMAL: Are you embarrassed to introduce me?

TAWFIQ: *No.* Look—never mind the meeting. I'll reschedule it for later. *(He starts heading for an exit.)* We can just go straight to the masjid.

*(*TAWFIQ *exits.* KAMAL *turns to* MONA.*)*

KAMAL: What's going on?

MONA: Nothing. It was a drama professor. Not engineering.

KAMAL: Drama? I'm paying for drama?

MONA: He's thinking of taking a course. It's a phase.

KAMAL: Life is drama enough. Why take a course in it?

(MONA *goes up to* KAMAL.)

KAMAL: He wants to be an actor?

MONA: No.

KAMAL: He'll starve. He'll never get cast.

MONA: Whatever he says to you—be patient. Don't explode.

KAMAL: I never explode. I just speak clearly. And loudly.

MONA: He doesn't know what he wants right now. Don't push him into making a decision he'll regret.

KAMAL: What are you hiding? I know when you're hiding something you don't want me to hear.

(MONA *makes some mollifying gesture, such as taking her husband's face in her hands, or touching his arm.*)

MONA: We've done well so far, haven't we? —Let's be thankful for what we have. Okay?

KAMAL: I am not going to like this, am I.

MONA: No. —I don't think you will.

(*Blackout*)

Scene 2

(*Lights dim. Several figures are present wearing some variation of extremely conservative veiling, where, in addition to the flowing robes, the faces are covered. These figures enter and stand at various points on the stage.*)

(Two chairs are placed on one side of the stage, perhaps, where PAULINE *is seated, and* HUWAIDA *stands nearby. Spot on this area of the stage.* HUWAIDA *is veiled but in a much more relaxed way: her face exposed. She wears jeans, or something equally casual.)*

HUWAIDA: Okay. So this is the dream. It's a dream, okay, so it's going to sound really, really weird.

PAULINE: That's alright. Go on. You've had this dream before?

HUWAIDA: Yes, and I'm sick of it; and I want to answer it back. I want to figure out what it wants to tell me so maybe it will go away. It's obvious to me on one level, but…. Do you believe dreams try to teach us things?

PAULINE: Sometimes. Why don't you tell me about it.

HUWAIDA: This is my first time with a psychologist.

PAULINE: I'm glad you came.

HUWAIDA: Just so you know. I'm not having a breakdown. I need someone to help me figure this out, that's all. Is this going in some record?

PAULINE: Everything said here is kept in strict confidence.

HUWAIDA: I don't want my parents to know.

PAULINE: They won't. You're perfectly safe here. Why don't you tell me about the dream.

HUWAIDA: Okay. *(Takes a breath)* So…there are these veiled figures.

(Lights up on the veiled figures)

HUWAIDA: Around five or six of them. Sometimes more. Sometimes it's a whole crowd. And they're just standing there, very still. And then I realize what they're doing. They're watching television. On a big screen.

(Perhaps a flickering light is shone on the figures to suggest a television set playing off-stage.)

HUWAIDA: And what they're watching is the Miss America contest. They're glued to the screen watching this…Miss America contest. And there's this feeling in the room that something terrible is about to happen. And then it does. And what happens is me. I'm in the contest. I'm a contestant in this beauty pageant. And for some reason it always begins in the swimsuit section. And it's like I'm both in the room watching, and on the screen waiting to come on. And I realize now these figures are not strangers, but my friends and relatives, people from the community. They've all gathered to watch me come out. And I do. I'm standing there, horrified, as I watch myself come out in a swimsuit.

(HUWAIDA's DOUBLE—H D—enters dressed in a one-piece swimsuit, carrying a beach-ball.)

HUWAIDA: And I'm veiled.

(H D wears a scarf that leaves her face exposed.)

HUWAIDA: It's bad enough I'm in a swimsuit. But on top of that I'm also veiled. Like I have to humiliate myself in front of Muslims and non-Muslims alike, like I'm a circus freak.

PAULINE: When you say veiled—

HUWAIDA: Just my hair. The rest of me is barely covered. Though I have to say, I look really good. The swimsuit fits fantastically on me. I mean I'm mortified but a part of me takes note of, wow: I'm not bad. That diet really worked. I should say of course that this woman, though I know it's me, looks nothing like me. Only it is me in the way you know it is in dreams. Anyway, I come out…and stand there with this stupid beach ball and smile.

(A spotlight up on H D, perhaps.)

HUWAIDA: One of those smiles only beauty contestants can get away with.

PAULINE: How do these figures react?

(The VEILED FIGURES *gasp in unison.)*

HUWAIDA: The expression "cut the air with a knife" comes to mind. There's enough outrage in the room to start a bonfire. And then out of nowhere a microphone is placed in front of me.

(During the above speech, a microphone on a stand has been placed before H D, or perhaps one is lowered from the ceiling.)

VEILED FIGURE 1: Oh no. She's going to speak.

H D: What did you think: I was just going to come out here and look beautiful?

HUWAIDA: And there's nothing I can do to shut myself up.

H D: I would like to dedicate this moment to all my Muslim sisters around the world.

HUWAIDA: Oh no.

H D: And to all my Muslim brothers I say, "salaam 'alaykum", and please hold off on your objections until after you see me in the talent section.

HUWAIDA: I get nauseous just telling you about it.

VEILED FIGURES: *(In unison, to* HUWAIDA*)* How could you do this to us?

HUWAIDA: *(To the* VEILED FIGURES*)* I had no idea I'd be in this contest, I swear to God.

H D: I think it's time we Muslims stepped out into the light and made a big splash. For too long we have let others misrepresent us, mock our ways and call us everything under the sun. Well I say, enough of that.

We're here, we're proud, and by golly we can kick ass along with the best of them.

HUWAIDA: *(To* H D*)* But you're in the swimsuit section, for crying out loud. What are you talking about?

H D: And another thing.

HUWAIDA: Oh no, please shut up.

H D: I am tired of being told that I have no modesty in coming out like this. I do have modesty. I was actually thinking of coming out in a bikini. Unfortunately I couldn't find one in the color I wanted. But isn't this great? *(Refers to the one-piece she's wearing)* My auntie made it for me. Auntie? *(She turns around to one of the* VEILED FIGURES *in the room.)* Would you like to take a bow.

(No one moves.)

H D: Go on. Don't be shy. Your work deserves praise.

(The VEILED FIGURES *turn to one particular figure. This* FIGURE *hesitates, then shrugs.)*

VEILED FIGURE 2: She's my niece. She asked. What could I say?

VEILED FIGURES: *(In unison) Shameless.*

HUWAIDA: *(To* PAULINE*)* And that's the end of the dream.

H D: No it's not. I haven't sung yet.

HUWAIDA: *(To* H D*)* I'm sorry, you're done.

H D: And I haven't made my speech about making the world a better place.

HUWAIDA: Please get off the stage.

H D: Or the line of swimsuits I want to open up for Muslim ladies on Venice Beach.

HUWAIDA: *(To off-stage crew)* Shut the microphone off right now. *(To the* VEILED FIGURES*)* That's all I'm telling about the dream. Get out. Please. Thank you.

(The VEILED FIGURES *exit.)*

H D: You are wound up way too tight.

HUWAIDA: That's why I'm here. Please just leave.

H D: 'Til tonight. And in the next dream, I'm singing. I'm thinking of doing the call to prayer in a funky pop tune with a good solid base.

HUWAIDA: *Get out.*

H D: *(As she exits, under her breath)* You're such a nutcase.

(H D's gone. Light change.)

HUWAIDA: *(To* PAULINE*)* I wake up in a sweat. And afterwards I can't sleep. This has been going on off and on for the past couple of months and I'm fed up. I can't…. It's like I can never grab a hold of it long enough to figure out what it wants.

PAULINE: You said it was obvious to you on one level, how?

HUWAIDA: Well—because…probably a part of me, even though I think it's a joke—maybe I'm a…closet exhibitionist or something. Or vain, and this dream is acting out what I don't permit myself in real life.

PAULINE: What don't you permit yourself?

HUWAIDA: I'd never be that…in-your-face. Or dumb, for that matter. I'd never degrade myself in that way. I'm a bit of a feminist, believe it or not.

PAULINE: But you take note in the dream that you look good.

HUWAIDA: Well heck, it's my dream, I might as well look good.

PAULINE: Why do you think you're also veiled?

HUWAIDA: Because it's still me; I suppose. I can't leave myself behind completely.

PAULINE: Is that how you identify yourself? As a veiled woman?

HUWAIDA: No. It's just what comes naturally. What makes sense.

PAULINE: Was veiling your choice?

HUWAIDA: You know, that's not relevant. What I want to know is—in your experienced, professional opinion, what comes to mind? What's up with this dream?

PAULINE: Huwaida: the question is what does it mean for you?

HUWAIDA: Oh no, don't do that. Don't throw it back to me. Is this what all psychologists do? Question your questions? So that you come out with more questions than you came in with?

PAULINE: Yes. And hopefully those additional inquiries help open up the problem that brought you in here. The idea being to leave you with a better grasp of what's going on. —Can I ask what your major is?

HUWAIDA: Why? —Mathematics.

PAULINE: Do you enjoy that?

HUWAIDA: I do. There are only so many interpretations you can make with numbers.

PAULINE: Was that your choice?

HUWAIDA: That's the second time you've asked me that. Yes it was. I'm also minoring in art.

PAULINE: Oh?

HUWAIDA: I come from a family of frustrated artists. My father was a calligrapher once. Now he sells carpets. I have to go.

(HUWAIDA *moves to the chair to get her backpack and jacket.*)

PAULINE: We still have the rest of the hour.

(HUWAIDA *starts putting away her schedule book, water bottle, and anything else she might have taken out.*)

HUWAIDA: I have to get ready for class.

PAULINE: I'd like to help you.

HUWAIDA: If you're just going to ask me questions, I can puzzle through the dream on my own. I was hoping for something else. Something a little more concrete, to make it stop.

PAULINE: Will you allow me one more question?

HUWAIDA: I really do need to go.

PAULINE: You said it was the Miss America contest? This will sound odd, but—do you know what state you were representing?

HUWAIDA: Excuse me?

PAULINE: On the sash. What did it say? California? New York?

HUWAIDA: What does that have to do with anything?

PAULINE: I was just wondering. Who were you representing?

(*In spite of the perceived silliness of the question,* HUWAIDA *stops to recall.*)

HUWAIDA: I...I didn't...

(H D *comes out again and stands near the wings. As before, she isn't wearing a sash. She begins to bounce the beach ball. Huwaida is looking at her.*)

HUWAIDA: I don't remember. I wasn't wearing one.

PAULINE: Were you representing anything? If not a state, something else? A country? A religion? I guess

I'm suggesting, and it's only a suggestion—that maybe
you're not wearing a sash because—in a sense...is the
veil the sash? Do you think?

H D: *(To* HUWAIDA*)* You are so lame.

PAULINE: Does it stand in for the sash? In the dream it's
clear who you address.

HUWAIDA: I knew you'd reduce it to that.

PAULINE: Reduce it to what?

HUWAIDA: "If she's having problems it has to be
because she's veiled."

PAULINE: I don't know if it is. Is it?

H D: Something's going to break, Huwaida.

HUWAIDA: Maybe my dream is a celebration of being
veiled. Inappropriate maybe, in the way dreams are,
but a celebration nonetheless, a coming out.

PAULINE: How can it be a celebration if your reaction is
one of embarrassment?

HUWAIDA: Well a part of me is enjoying it.

PAULINE: The other half is mortified.

HUWAIDA: Well I guess that's life? We're always
splitting off into different people depending on the
occasion.

PAULINE: Yes. And a healthy person is one who is able
to integrate those various parts.

H D: Why don't you tell her what's going on.

PAULINE: Did you choose to be veiled?

HUWAIDA: *(To* H D*)* Would you stop bouncing that
ball!

(H D *stops; to* PAULINE*;)*

HUWAIDA: Look. I don't need to be liberated, or saved. I just want this annoying character in my dream to go away.

PAULINE: Let's work on it.

HUWAIDA: I don't think so. I came to see a psychologist, not an anthropologist.

PAULINE: Are you sure it's not you who's starting to look at yourself in an awkward way?

HUWAIDA: Sorry, but you're way off. I have to go. *(She heads for the door.)*

PAULINE: Huwaida.

H D: Huwaida! Catch!

(H D throws the beach ball to HUWAIDA, *who catches it. Blackout)*

Scene 3

(In the blackout we hear the call to prayer. Lights up on an area outside the mosque.)

*(*TAWFIQ *enters holding his shoes. He stops at a spot and starts putting them on.* HAMZA *comes out. At some point during the scene he will also start putting on his shoes.)*

HAMZA: What happened?

(No response)

HAMZA: What's up?

TAWFIQ: And you? How are you doing?

HAMZA: Why weren't you praying? ...Why were you just standing there like that?

TAWFIQ: Well, let's see. I was just standing there probably because I wasn't praying. Or, I wasn't praying because I couldn't figure out what I was doing standing there. What were you doing? As someone who was praying. Perhaps you can clue me in.

HAMZA: What's up?

TAWFIQ: What's up? I guess that's what I can't figure out. Which takes me back to why I was just standing there.

HAMZA: Seriously, man, what's going on?

TAWFIQ: Why is it whenever anyone asks me that question and I tell them, it's as if they haven't heard me. *(Spelling it out)* I wasn't praying because I didn't want to. I do not want to pray. I did not want to come to the mosque. I chickened out and came anyway because God forbid we should upset Puppy. God forbid we should have our own opinions and beliefs.

HAMZA: What do you mean you don't want to pray?

TAWFIQ: It's just amazing how people can't get their minds around this. *Figure it out.*

HAMZA: Why are you so pissed off? —Really. You've been acting ticked off for weeks.

TAWFIQ: Yeah, well, things change.

HAMZA: Like what? —Talk to me, man.

TAWFIQ: Talk to you? You really want me to do that?

HAMZA: When did you stop believing in God?

TAWFIQ: What are *you* doing in there?

HAMZA: I mean it, man. All of a sudden?

TAWFIQ: I'll tell you when. When I did what God commands all of us to do: to open our eyes and look around us. Investigate; question. I took those commands very seriously. I questioned, I looked. Unfortunately I questioned him right out of existence.

HAMZA: Oh yeah? How'd you do that?

TAWFIQ: Have you even bothered to think about this? Or do you just go in there 'cause it's what our father does?

HAMZA: Are you embarrassed to be a Muslim now?

TAWFIQ: Oh, please. It has nothing to do with that.

HAMZA: Is all this crap they're saying about us getting to you?

TAWFIQ: That's not the reason; if anything, it's what's kept me a Muslim this long.

HAMZA: You're not going to change your name on us now are you?

(TAWFIQ *goes up to* HAMZA.)

TAWFIQ: Tell me something. Are you sure the God in there loves you?

HAMZA: What does that have to do with anything?

TAWFIQ: It's a pretty basic question, don't you think?

HAMZA: Yes, I know He does.

TAWFIQ: If you strictly follow certain things. Certain basic things.

HAMZA: That's right. As with every faith.

TAWFIQ: Like who you love, and how you love.

HAMZA: Among other things.

TAWFIQ: Conditional love. God's love is conditional. I love you unconditionally, and somehow God's love is less than mine? Does that make sense? That my love should be bigger than his?

HAMZA: No: what it says, it's repeated enough times is, the "All Merciful, the Compassionate."

TAWFIQ: As long as you play by his rules.

HAMZA: That would follow, sure; why does that sound strange to you?

TAWFIQ: It just seems very petty. If you're going to be God, don't you think your capacity to love and forgive should be bigger than ours?

HAMZA: It is; the rules are guidelines, to support you.

TAWFIQ: They're more than guidelines. These are player's rules. Break one and you're that much closer to getting kicked out of the game permanently.

HAMZA: You don't think we need help? I'm not so arrogant as to believe I've got it all figured out. And the other way is what? No laws? We're too weak for that.

TAWFIQ: Yes, we're human. I don't want to be penalized for being human.

HAMZA: God allows for our weaknesses.

TAWFIQ: Up to a point. After that it's "burn, baby, burn".

HAMZA: Why are you focusing on the negatives? It's such a small part.

TAWFIQ: People going to hell? That's a detail to you?

HAMZA: There have to be consequences, in everything. And the Qur'an repeatedly speaks of forgiving sins. And why would you cut yourself off from His blessings?

TAWFIQ: Because I don't believe he exists to give me any!

(Beat)

HAMZA: When'd you start believing all this?

TAWFIQ: Is that how you classify it? A weakness?

HAMZA: What?

TAWFIQ: I'm just wondering. —Where you stand? — Where—if something feels so right—and good—it makes you glow inside, and gives meaning to your

life like nothing else does. And you know in your
heart this can't be a sin. It can't be because it feels too
necessary just to breathe. And it doesn't hurt anybody,
and it is good and it just has to be. What if your faith
forbids it? What then? ...What do you do then?

HAMZA: What are you talking about?

(TAWFIQ *looks at* HAMZA *for a moment, then turns and
walks away.*)

HAMZA: Where are you going? ...Tawfiq. Wait up.

(TAWFIQ *has exited.* HAMZA *stands there for a moment.*
KAMAL *enters carrying his shoes, the oud, and a backpack.*)

KAMAL: Did he leave?

HAMZA: He had a...he had an appointment.

KAMAL: *(Referring to the backpack)* He forgot this.

HAMZA: I can take it to him.

KAMAL: You go practice. When he remembers he'll
come back for it. *(He hands* HAMZA *the oud)* What's
wrong with him?

HAMZA: *(Shrugs)* I don't know, he's... He seems to be...
He didn't really say.

(Slight beat)

KAMAL: So far everyone in this family knows what's
going on except me. Why is that? Is it so difficult to tell
me things? —Never mind. Go practice. I'll see you at
"iftar".

HAMZA: Do you want me to bring anything on the way
back?

KAMAL: Call your mother, see if she needs anything.

HAMZA: Okay...I'll see you later.

(HAMZA starts to walk off. KAMAL *sits to put on his shoes.)*
KAMAL: Hamza.

(HAMZA *stops*)

KAMAL: Is everything alright?

HAMZA: Yes.

KAMAL: Don't you kiss your father goodbye anymore?

HAMZA: Oh. *(Goes over to his father)* Sorry.

KAMAL: You can't forget these things with me. I'm very sensitive.

(HAMZA *leans down to kiss* KAMAL. KAMAL *holds him for a second as he affectionately pats his cheek.)*

KAMAL: I'm very proud of you.

HAMZA: *(Feeling awkward)* Thanks.

KAMAL: If you see people around you doing this: *(He puts his fingers in his ears.)* come home. *(Takes fingers out)* We understand your sounds better than they do.

HAMZA: *(Smiling)* I'll do that. I'll see you later.

(HAMZA *starts to exit.* KAMAL *continues tying up his shoes.)*

KAMAL: You'll be a good musician one day. Don't give up.

HAMZA: *(Just before he exits)* I won't.

KAMAL: *(To himself)* "Inshallah...Inshallah."

(TAWFIQ *enters. Sees* KAMAL; *hesitates; then comes forward.)*

TAWFIQ: Hi.

KAMAL: "Salaam 'alaykum."

TAWFIQ: Forgot my bag.

KAMAL: Yes you did.

(TAWFIQ *picks up his backpack but* KAMAL *grabs hold of the other end.)*

KAMAL: You also forgot to say goodbye.

TAWFIQ: I'm late for a meeting.

KAMAL: Your teacher?

TAWFIQ: No; someone else.

KAMAL: Are you not feeling well?

TAWFIQ: I'm fine.

KAMAL: So you behaved that way inside why? ...We can have this conversation now; or we can have it later. But we will have it. *(He lets go of the bag.)* Your mother thinks I will be upset with your news. What upsets me is being treated like I can't handle the problems of my children. Like I'm a guest in my own family who mustn't be allowed to know too much. *(If he's finished tying his shoes, perhaps he stands up at this point.)* If it is bad news, it is better said than left to stay secret and become something it needn't be, no?

TAWFIQ: I don't want to come to the mosque again.

KAMAL: *(Slight beat)* That's the big news?

TAWFIQ: Yes.

KAMAL: No problem. Is that all?

TAWFIQ: And I don't consider myself a Muslim anymore.

KAMAL: Oh.... Okay.

TAWFIQ: I think God's a joke.... I mean...you're welcome to believe in him.... But I don't.

KAMAL: *(Slight beat)* Uh-huh.... Is there more?

(TAWFIQ shakes his head.)

KAMAL: Will you be joining us for "iftar"?

TAWFIQ: I don't know yet.

(Slight beat)

KAMAL: Anything else?

TAWFIQ: No.

(Slight beat)

KAMAL: Can we still hug? Or don't you believe in that anymore?

TAWFIQ: This isn't a phase. I'm not just going through something and will come to my senses later. It's what I believe.

KAMAL: Did I say anything? You are free to believe what you want. I'm just asking for a hug.

TAWFIQ: You want to dismiss what I just said.

KAMAL: What do you want me to do? Get angry?

*(*TAWFIQ *turns and starts to leave.)*

KAMAL: *(Quiet)* You do not walk away from me like that. Ever.

*(*TAWFIQ *has turned to look at* KAMAL.*)*

TAWFIQ: I'm late. I'm sorry. *(He turns and exits.)*

KAMAL: Tawfiq...Tawfiq!

(Blackout)

Scene 4

(Lights up on the living room. KAMAL *will step into the living room and stand there for a few beats. He has his shoes off again. The space is still empty of furniture. There are scuff marks on the floor, as if people have been walking all over it. He stares at the floor.)*

KAMAL: Anyone home? *(Louder)* Mona?

MONA: *(Off-stage)* I'm in the kitchen.

KAMAL: Please come out here.

MONA: I'm busy.

KAMAL: Mona!

(Slight beat. MONA *appears at the doorway.)*

MONA: I didn't hear you come in. *(Sees floor, gasps)* What did you do?

KAMAL: What did *I* do?

MONA: It was drying.

KAMAL: I just got here. I found it like this.

MONA: You didn't do this?

KAMAL: No. I just got here. Doesn't anyone have any sense around here? Who did this?

MONA: It doesn't matter. Let's just clean it up. *(She exits.)*

KAMAL: Of course it matters. It matters if our children have become so irresponsible they don't know how to behave.

MONA: *(Off-stage)* Kamal, it's the floor. It's dirt, it's not a crisis. *(She re-enters with a mop.)*

KAMAL: It tells me they have no respect for anything anymore. Were you here the entire time?

MONA: Don't worry about it.

KAMAL: Why should you mop the floor? Leave it. It's not your mess.

MONA: I want to do it.

KAMAL: Let one of them do it.

MONA: I've already started.

*(*KAMAL *moves to take the mop away from* MONA.*)*

KAMAL: I'm fed up of you making excuses for them all the time.

MONA: And I'm tired of not having any furniture to sit on!

(Slight beat as KAMAL *and* MONA *both hold onto the mop)*

MONA: Let me just finish.

KAMAL: I'll do it.

MONA: As you wish.

*(*KAMAL *takes the mop from* MONA *and starts vigorously cleaning the floor for a few beats before throwing the mop to the floor. They stand there for a moment.)*

KAMAL: It was a mistake coming to this country.

MONA: Twenty-five years later, this is the conclusion you come to?

(Slight beat)

KAMAL: Why did we come? —So I could sell carpets? —This is my great accomplishment?

(Slight beat)

MONA: They're beautiful carpets.

KAMAL: They're carpets.

MONA: They bought this house.

KAMAL: They're still carpets.

MONA: They put our children through school. Good schools.

KAMAL: Not good enough.

MONA: He spoke to you?

KAMAL: It would never have happened if we'd stayed.

MONA: What did he say?

KAMAL: We have a responsibility for what goes on inside here also. *(He presses his hand against his chest)*

MONA: What did he say?

KAMAL: He didn't want to…he didn't want to hug me. His own father.

MONA: What do you mean?

KAMAL: I opened my arms to him and he refused.

MONA: *(Slight beat)* How did you do it?

KAMAL: What do you mean, how did I do it?

MONA: How did you do it?

KAMAL: *(He opens his arms as if for an embrace)* Like this. Normal.

MONA: Are you sure it wasn't like that? *(She also opens her arms for an embrace but with a slightly more aggressive stance.)*

KAMAL: What is that?

MONA: This is "hug me or else".

KAMAL: I don't do that. That's you.

MONA: I'm your wife, I like them. But maybe your children find it too much.

KAMAL: Oh this is when you become impossible, when you defend your children to a ridiculous point.

MONA: He's trying to grow up. *(At some point during the following speech, she will pick up the mop and start cleaning.)*

KAMAL: Being disrespectful and rude is growing up? Or is that what growing up means in this country? Treating your parents like they are something that has fallen out of fashion. And while we're about it, let's throw God out too, because he doesn't go with all the latest trends either. He isn't cool enough. Isn't hip enough. He asks too much, demands too much. Takes away from one's busy schedule of shopping, and watching more T V, and everything else people feel they must do to function—to be considered a healthy member of this society. *That's what being healthy means here.* And God has no place in it. This is the environment we brought Tawfiq up in. We should've stayed put!

MONA: Kamal: he turned out fine. They all did, "Alhamdulillah". He's just trying to be his own man. You did it when you went against your father's wishes and came here.

KAMAL: And look at the good it did me; I should've listened.

MONA: Yes, look at the good, let us be thankful.

KAMAL: And I did not part on bad terms. I came to him and talked about it. I treated him with respect, in the way parents everywhere are treated except here.

MONA: Kamal, please, it's not the end of the world. He's free to see things the way he wants to. Let him stumble forward on his own.

KAMAL: And if his stumbling leads him to the edge of a cliff, are we supposed to stand back and watch him fall? Don't we have a responsibility for his soul? And what if it's not a phase and he has stopped believing?

MONA: Then he has stopped believing. What are we supposed to do, shove God down his throat? He doesn't believe in Him and that's that. He knows where He is if he changes his mind.

KAMAL: This doesn't sadden you?

(If MONA *hasn't stopped mopping before, perhaps she stops now.)*

MONA: Why? I have no reason to be sad. I have a beautiful daughter who is getting engaged tomorrow; who has no problem being a Muslim and fitting into this country. I have a son who is more curious about the country we came from than we ever were. And yes, we have a son who has decided he can live just fine without being a Muslim. And so what? He's not an addict; he's not lazy; it's not because he wants to live a crazy life and do depraved things.

KAMAL: We don't know that.

MONA: Oh stop.

KAMAL: We may yet find this out.

MONA: Whatever else he is, he is responsible and wants to make something of himself. I have a hundred reasons to be thankful, and so do you. Here, finish please. *(Holds out the mop)* I have to start the soup for Aziz. Was Murad there?

KAMAL: *(Takes the mop)* This is like Afifi. Exactly. Becoming a Christian. Wanting to call herself Sandra.

MONA: That was different. She was getting married.

KAMAL: But why become a Christian? Her husband didn't care. He would've converted.

MONA: Because it's Afifi. She likes to be dramatic.

KAMAL: *Because it was an easy way out.* Being a Muslim in this country has become too difficult now. Too many complications. Nobody wants to take the trouble to actually live their faith.

MONA: Forget Afifi and finish the floor. *(She starts to exit.)*

KAMAL: It's Sandra not Afifi. And when Tawfiq becomes Tom, will that be alright with you? Will we lose him piece by piece?

MONA: *(Faces KAMAL)* When he comes home tonight, please—I don't want to argue about this; or even talk about it. If you start, it will explode, you know it will. Tomorrow is a special day. Please, let's have peace in this house. Promise me this won't become something it doesn't have to be.

(KAMAL has resumed mopping)

MONA: Kamal, promise me.

KAMAL: I heard you...go finish what you were doing.

(MONA *remains where she is*)

KAMAL: I heard you!

(*Slight beat.* MONA *turns and exits.* KAMAL *continues mopping before he suddenly hurls the mop away. He stands there as the lights quickly fade to black.*)

Scene 5

(*Secluded courtyard on campus. Lights up on* TAWFIQ, *waiting, his backpack at his feet.* HUWAIDA *enters carrying her own backpack.*)

HUWAIDA: What is so important I have to be late for my class?

TAWFIQ: You hate that class. You should thank me.

HUWAIDA: I still have to pass it.

TAWFIQ: What's to learn? It's an art class.

HUWAIDA: What do you want, Tawfiq?

TAWFIQ: To say hi. We haven't said hi in weeks.

HUWAIDA: Bye. (*She starts to leave.*)

TAWFIQ: Huwaida.

HUWAIDA: I have work to do.

TAWFIQ: I want to talk to you.

HUWAIDA: What about? You've made yourself so very clear on every subject.

TAWFIQ: We're not on speaking terms now?

HUWAIDA: You? Mr Sphinx? Mr Don't-Talk-To-Me-I'm-Too-Busy-Being-Special? You're such a hypocrite.

TAWFIQ: I told Puppy...I told him.

HUWAIDA: Told him what?

TAWFIQ: You know...about...not being a Muslim anymore.

(Slight beat as HUWAIDA *stares at* TAWFIQ.*)*

HUWAIDA: When?

TAWFIQ: A little while ago. At the masjid.

HUWAIDA: You told him?

TAWFIQ: Yes. I finally had the guts to say it the way I feel it.

(Slight beat)

HUWAIDA: You asshole.

TAWFIQ: Thanks.

HUWAIDA: How did he react?

TAWFIQ: I don't know that he believes me.

HUWAIDA: Good, that's the way it'll stay.

TAWFIQ: No, it needs to be made very clear.

HUWAIDA: You promised you weren't going to bring this up until after the engagement. Now he's going to be ticked off, you little shit. Why did you tell him?

TAWFIQ: It came up.

HUWAIDA: Oh, bull, you deliberately told him.

TAWFIQ: I don't want to walk around like I'm a criminal in my own home.

HUWAIDA: You can be so destructive.

TAWFIQ: What is wrong with being honest?

HUWAIDA: That's not being honest. That's wanting everything to stop and pay attention to you. Well congratulations, you've soured everything.

TAWFIQ: I'm looking out for you, Huwaida, believe it or not. I want what's best.

HUWAIDA: Precisely. Thank you. That's why you told him. You want to screw up the engagement, well give up. It's going to happen.

TAWFIQ: Huwaida: I really want you to think about what you're doing.

(Reacting to a look:)

TAWFIQ: I'm not going to stand by and watch you do something I know you'll regret.

HUWAIDA: You know what really ticks me off about atheists, if that's what you are. They make the worse zealots. They walk around with contempt for anyone who might be stupid enough to believe something they don't. Like suddenly you're plugged into something we mere mortals struggling in the dark could never imagine. And it's your duty to enlighten us and you won't stop until we bow down before your own private temple of reason and give up our stupid beliefs. You're worse than the fanatics. You and all fundamentalists should find yourselves a nice little island and preach yourselves to death.

TAWFIQ: You think what you're doing is enlightened?

HUWAIDA: Are you going to live my life for me?

TAWFIQ: Don't do this to please mom and dad.

HUWAIDA: They're the ones who argued against it!

TAWFIQ: Oh come on, you know they were thrilled, in spite of what they said. Mother's been pushing this guy on you for years.

HUWAIDA: *Just stay out of it.*

TAWFIQ: I know you're having second thoughts about this and don't want to admit it.

HUWAIDA: Oh, *now* you know what goes on in my head? Are those special powers that come with being an atheist?

TAWFIQ: Stand outside of this for one second: don't you think what you're doing is bizarre? By any standards?

HUWAIDA: Are you aware that over half the marriages in this country fail. Leaving a miserable trail of step parents and screwed-up kids. As opposed to arranged marriages that have a much higher success rate.

TAWFIQ: Tell me you're happy going into this.

HUWAIDA: You wouldn't believe me if I said yes.

TAWFIQ: Because I don't believe *you* believe it. You're so stubborn you'd rather plow on ahead than admit you've made a huge mistake.

HUWAIDA: I want to get married! How much clearer do I have to be?

TAWFIQ: Fine. But at least meet the man you're going to marry.

HUWAIDA: I will be meeting him! I'll have the rest of my life to meet him and get to know him.

(Slight beat)

TAWFIQ: This is just too crazy. Nobody does this anymore. Not even in Egypt.

HUWAIDA: It's a lot saner than strangers hooking up on-line, which you have no problem with.

TAWFIQ: What are you trying to prove? How pious you are?

HUWAIDA: Tawfiq…I can't explain it further. I just know this is the best thing for me. I really do. I know it in my bones.

(Slight beat)

TAWFIQ: Aren't you nervous?

HUWAIDA: *Yes.* Of course I'm nervous. I'm…a part of me's petrified.

TAWFIQ: Why not listen to that part of you?

HUWAIDA: Because I *know*. Yes, even in my heart I know.

(Slight beat)

TAWFIQ: You grew up to be very odd, you know that.

*(*HUWAIDA *picks up her backpack as she gets ready to leave.)*

HUWAIDA: If you're not going to support me, at least don't interfere. Besides, he's not a stranger. I've spoken to him enough times on the phone.

TAWFIQ: Huwaida: promise me one thing. *(Turns to a corner and waves his arms)* If you see him and don't like him, don't go through with it.

HUWAIDA: What are you doing?

TAWFIQ: Get his vibe, talk to him, and if anything seems odd, cancel it. I'll back you up.

HUWAIDA: Who are you waving to?

TAWFIQ: I invited him here.

HUWAIDA: Who?

TAWFIQ: Murad.

HUWAIDA: You invited him?

TAWFIQ: He wants to meet you.

HUWAIDA: You invited him here? *(Looks in the direction* TAWFIQ *waved)* You shit. Why'd you do that?

TAWFIQ: So if a face-to-face meeting bombs, you don't have to go through with it.

HUWAIDA: You are such an asshole.

TAWFIQ: Related to you by blood, which makes me a loving and caring asshole.

HUWAIDA: I'm not properly dressed.

TAWFIQ: You're gorgeous.

HUWAIDA: I don't want him to see me like this. I swear to God I'm going to kill you.

TAWFIQ: Thou shalt not kill your sibling, especially when he's trying to help you.

(HUWAIDA *tries to bolt;* TAWFIQ *blocks her way.*)

TAWFIQ: What are you afraid of? That you'll see him and not like him? Good. There's every chance you won't. He doesn't have a clue about your life here.

(MURAD *appears. The brother and sister turn to him.* TAWFIQ *speaks to* HUWAIDA, *not caring if* MURAD *overhears.*)

TAWFIQ: You don't have to do this. —Any of it. *(He turns to* MURAD, *nods his head; back to his sister.)* I'll see you later.

(TAWFIQ *exits.* HUWAIDA *is staring at* MURAD, *looking somewhat paralyzed. When* MURAD *speaks it is with an accent.)*

MURAD: Your brother phoned me.... He said...that you wanted to see me?

(Slight beat)

HUWAIDA: No...I don't.

MURAD: *(Slight beat)* Oh.

HUWAIDA: I mean...this is fine.... I just didn't know you were coming.

MURAD: You would like me to leave?

HUWAIDA: Would you mind?

MURAD: *(Slight beat)* You...*do* want me to...?

HUWAIDA: Unless you want to stay, I could go.

MURAD: No, I will go.

HUWAIDA: No. Since my brother dragged you here, you should stay.

MURAD: Not at all. I will find my way back.

HUWAIDA: I insist; it's a nice campus. Walk around. I have a class.

MURAD: Ah.

HUWAIDA: Yes, I have an art class. Otherwise I'd stay.

(Beat)

MURAD: I am happy we finally….

HUWAIDA: Yes… Nice to meet you too. *(She goes up to him and somewhat formerly shakes his hand.)* Welcome to the States. I'm sorry for the misunderstanding.

MURAD: It is not a problem.

HUWAIDA: Plus I'm very sweaty.

MURAD: Excuse me?

HUWAIDA: The, um. I'm not—. These are pretty ratty clothes. I didn't want you to— …This really isn't how I wanted our first meeting to go.

MURAD: *(Not getting what she means)* I…

HUWAIDA: *(Points to a hole in her clothing)* Look: it has a hole. In case you've seen it and think, "Gee, that says a lot. What kind of wife will she be if she goes around with holes in her clothing." I'm aware of it. And the sneakers have clearly died on me, I know that too except I haven't had time to go shopping, and I know my face must look all puffed up because when I run around, that's what happens, I puff up. Plus anytime I have an annoying conversation with my brother, I break into hives. How's your father?

MURAD: He is better, thank you.

HUWAIDA: Will he be coming tomorrow?

MURAD: Inshallah.

HUWAIDA: Inshallah. *(Slight beat)* I'm...sorry we haven't been able to meet.

MURAD: You have exams?

HUWAIDA: Well, between classes and Ramadan—and running around, it's been—hectic.

MURAD: Yes.

HUWAIDA: *(Slight beat)* Did it seem weird to you that I didn't call?

MURAD: *(Smiles, shrugs)* I...

HUWAIDA: Did you want to see me?

MURAD: Of course.

HUWAIDA: Why?

MURAD: Because...we're getting engaged?

HUWAIDA: Right. *(Slight beat)* You'd have preferred to spend some time together before?

MURAD: A walk or two would be nice.

HUWAIDA: *(Slight beat)* And yet you got on the plane and came all the way here to get engaged to a woman you barely know.

MURAD: Our families know each other.

HUWAIDA: But—you don't know me.

MURAD: I remember your visits.

HUWAIDA: I was six and thirteen. I've changed.

MURAD: Yes. You have. And yet...as it is said...the child is a parent to the adult that follows, no?

HUWAIDA: I've really changed.

MURAD: And you? It is a gamble for you too. To say yes to a man you know only through the phone. A picture.

HUWAIDA: True. —But in practice, it never seems to work out, does it. Getting to know the other person beforehand. You hear of people spending years together before they marry and then they do and it all falls apart. So what advantages did they have in getting to know each other? Perhaps that was the problem. They entered the marriage with nothing to give to each other by way of discovery. There was no mystery.

MURAD: You like mystery?

HUWAIDA: It's not that. It's just that I feel dating is overrated. —It gives you a false impression of knowing the other person, before entering into a commitment that by its nature changes the people who enter into it.... Which is to say you can't really know the person until you enter into that very thing that changes the both of you. That's when you really begin to see the other person. Do you see what I'm saying?

(MURAD *looks confused.*)

HUWAIDA: Which is why some people never get married, because they know it changes everything.

MURAD: The two people who marry will know each other soon enough. —The mystery is soon over.

HUWAIDA: Replaced by respect, hopefully. What you show of yourself in marriage, under the sacredness of those vows taken, and what you learn of the other person, acquire different meanings.... And the difficulties that naturally arise, which—obviously there are always problems, these are handled with your vows in mind. Those vows become the third party in any dispute, so to speak. —The sacredness of your commitment becomes—that becomes the mystery. (*Slight beat*) Do you...

(*Seeing that* MURAD *might not understand:*)

HUWAIDA: Do you see what I'm saying?

MURAD: Yes…. It is very interesting what you say.

HUWAIDA: Interesting?

MURAD: It is, yes.

HUWAIDA: But what do you think about what I just said? —You must have an opinion.

MURAD: I do.

HUWAIDA: Can I hear it?

MURAD: Wouldn't you prefer to wait until we get married?

(HUWAIDA *is not amused.*)

HUWAIDA: In other words you think what I was saying is stupid.

MURAD: Not at all. No. I have just not—I have never thought of it in this way.

HUWAIDA: You must share a similar viewpoint or you wouldn't be here.

MURAD: I am here…because of you.

HUWAIDA: What do you mean? —Yes, me; and what I believe, and what you believe. We've talked enough on the phone to know we at least share the same beliefs; care about the same things. You hear of people meeting, the chemistry's great and then after six months they break up. They discover they don't agree on anything, beyond the basic, "Do you find each other attractive?", and you're not too far from the pictures you sent me. So no shock there. Am I?

MURAD: *(Not following)* Are you what?

HUWAIDA: Am I like my photos?

MURAD: No.

HUWAIDA: I'm not?

MURAD: You are more beautiful.... Many times more attractive.

(Slight beat)

HUWAIDA: I paid three hundred dollars for those headshots.

MURAD: I apologize if I prefer the real person.

HUWAIDA: *(Slight beat)* I look horrible.

MURAD: Even better. Now I know when you look horrible, you are also beautiful.

HUWAIDA: Please don't feel you have to say these things.

MURAD: I want to say them.

HUWAIDA: Because one of the things that gets my goat is friends will go on about how their boyfriends said this and that to them and then later finding out these wonderful guys with their wonderful words were dishonest cheats. One of the benefits of doing this is not having to go through *that*. Pass stops A through Z and all the dating bull that goes with it.... Why are you looking at me like that?

MURAD: *(Not grasping the question)* Excuse me?

HUWAIDA: Why are you—staring at me like that?

MURAD: We are—meeting finally? —I'm sorry if my looking offends you.

HUWAIDA: It's not that. I'd just...I would prefer it if you'd please respond to what I've been saying.

MURAD: Which part?

HUWAIDA: Any part. Pick something.

MURAD: Yes. —I see. —I will tell you then.... I believe in mystery too. —Like you do.... I believe in love. —Like you must do. I believe if it is there, you do not need much to know it. A look. A photo. Even a

cheap one. A phone call. I believe the mystery never
disappears, if you don't want it to. And when people
get bored, it is by nothing that matters. By habits,
things that make them go to sleep and not see clearly
anymore the person they care about. And to change
this they only have to wake up and see again the
person they love to remember this mystery. That also
comes with its own...unexplainable solution, yes?
—And if it is there, this wonderful mystery, respect
follows. How can you not respect someone who opens
your eyes to something this good. Especially someone
who draws it out of you so easily. This is the wedding
gift, no? This is the contract. What we give to each
other. It is the only gift that matters.

HUWAIDA: *(Slight beat)* Please don't take this the wrong
way. —But I have to ask. So it's not this thing floating
in the back of my mind. Are you doing this to get a
green card? *(Slight beat)* Not that I believe it is, but,
obviously, the thought's occurred to me. And I'd just
like to get it out of the way.... There's no polite way of
asking.

(Slight beat)

MURAD: No. One of the obstacles to this union—was
that I might have to live here.

HUWAIDA: We *are* going to live here.

MURAD: I understand. But what I am saying—living
here is not the prize you think it is. You should also
know I'm not going to pursue my medical studies.

HUWAIDA: Oh? —What are you thinking of doing?

MURAD: I have not decided yet. I'm sorry you will not
be marrying a doctor.

HUWAIDA: I don't care about that.

MURAD: And I do not care about a green card.

HUWAIDA: But you have me worried now: can you see yourself living here?

MURAD: Yes; it is all the same.

HUWAIDA: No, it's not. It's not all the same.

MURAD: If I am comfortable with you, I will be comfortable where ever I live.

HUWAIDA: I don't know if that follows.... Are we crazy for doing this?

MURAD: It is natural to be scared. I am a little scared too.

HUWAIDA: What if it's too much of a shock to all you're used to?

MURAD: I am marrying *you*, Huwaida. It is you I see. And want.

HUWAIDA: But you don't know me. *How do you know?*

(MURAD *holds out his hand.*)

MURAD: For the same reason you do.

HUWAIDA: What if *I* don't know anymore.

MURAD: Let us see.

(HUWAIDA *doesn't take* MURAD's *hand. Slight beat*)

HUWAIDA: I really have to go.

(MURAD *withdraws his hand;* HUWAIDA *starts to go.*)

MURAD: Wait, please.

(HUWAIDA *stops.*)

MURAD: I will go. (*He takes a few steps towards her.*) I am sorry to have surprised you today. But...perhaps it is best I did. Do not worry. If it is God's will, this engagement will happen. Remember the thing that made you say yes to this. Perhaps it is a good voice that whispered to you.... I hope it is still whispering to you. (*Slight beat*) Enjoy your class.

(MURAD *exits.* HUWAIDA *remains where she is.*)

HUWAIDA: *(To herself)* Shit. *Shit.*

(Blackout)

Scene 6

(In the blackout, we hear the sounds of the oud. The music is a little more coherent and recognizable than before.)

(Lights up on a park area. HAMZA, wearing his skull-cap, is sitting on the park bench, practicing his oud. He stops and starts on a tune, trying to get it just right.)

(During the playing, a man—KEVIN—enters as if having heard the music from another area of the park. He hangs back, listening. When the tune ends, he claps. HAMZA turns, startled. KEVIN continues clapping as he approaches.)

KEVIN: Not bad…not bad at all.

HAMZA: *(Embarrassed)* No. Not really.

KEVIN: It was good.

HAMZA: Thanks, but.

KEVIN: I know that tune. What was it?

HAMZA: I don't think you could call that a tune. It was more like a bad pile up of notes.

KEVIN: Was that Cole Porter?

HAMZA: You actually heard a melody?

KEVIN: Where did you learn that?

HAMZA: Nowhere. —Myself. —If that isn't obvious.

KEVIN: Cole Porter on a oud. That's a first. I'm impressed.

HAMZA: You know ouds?

KEVIN: I'm a big fan of the oud.

HAMZA: Yeah? How come? They're not exactly popular.

KEVIN: I like mandolins. The oud gave birth to the mandolin. And lutes.

HAMZA: What's a lute?

KEVIN: It's sort of like that. A renaissance instrument. It's what the Europeans picked up from the Arabs. Among other things.

HAMZA: You know how to play?

KEVIN: Strictly an admirer. I like musical instruments in general. I find them fascinating.

HAMZA: If I could learn just one I'd be happy.

KEVIN: Why did you pick that?

HAMZA: It was in our basement. —It belonged to my grandfather. I just started playing it one day. And drove my family nuts.

KEVIN: Hey, it could've been worse. Your grandfather could've played the drums.

HAMZA: I think that's what they hear when I play.

KEVIN: Where are you from?

HAMZA: Originally? San Diego.

KEVIN: I mean—where's your family from?

HAMZA: Oh. —Egypt.

KEVIN: Wow. Always wanted to go…. I'd definitely buy a oud from there. Though I hear the best ones are found in Turkey. They use a different quality string, apparently.

HAMZA: You do know about ouds.

KEVIN: You like Cole Porter?

HAMZA: I can't say I know him. It's a tune I hear playing in my advisor's office every time I go see her.

KEVIN: Then you have a good ear, if you picked it up just like that. *(Slight beat)* Can I...can I hold it?

HAMZA: Er—sure. If you want.

KEVIN: *(Approaching)* I just love the way they look. And the feel of them. *(He takes the oud and positions it as if to play)* They're so unique. —I wish I could play.

HAMZA: Go ahead.

KEVIN: I respect music too much to butcher it.

HAMZA: It doesn't stop me.

KEVIN: That's why you're a musician and I'm not. I couldn't put up with the mistakes I'd have to make to become good. I just find it so bizarre how we decide what is music and what isn't. I mean why isn't this pleasing? *(He randomly strums the oud.)* Why not? Why is that noise and something else a tune? What makes us know that this note, and not that one needs to follow in order to make pleasing sounds. So even if it's a tune from another country and it sounds foreign, we can still recognize it as having—as being melodic.

(Slight beat)

HAMZA: Are you in the music business?

KEVIN: Nope. Studying law. No music there. Just arguments. And you?

HAMZA: I'm—I'm also a student.

KEVIN: Where?

HAMZA: At U S C.

KEVIN: What are you studying?

HAMZA: Computer Science.

KEVIN: Do you play here often?

HAMZA: No. It just seemed a quiet place. To practice.

(Slight beat)

KEVIN: Practice what?

HAMZA: Can I have my oud back?

(Slight beat)

KEVIN: You know, there's a funny myth attached to the invention of the oud. Do you know it?

(KEVIN holds out the oud. HAMZA takes it.)

HAMZA: No.

KEVIN: Well...it is said—the myth goes, that the oud was invented by Lamak, a direct descendant of Cain. The sixth grandson of Adam. And when Lamak's son died, he hung his remains on a tree, for some reason. And when the remains dried out, when they were completely desiccated, the skeleton suggested the form of the oud.... And from that moment on, God gave the sons of Cain the know-how to make musical instruments. And so...they did. Lamak invented the oud, the drum and the harp. And these instruments became celebrated for treating illnesses. For reviving the heart; invigorating the body. Creating balance. — Fascinating, huh? *(Extends his hand)* Kevin.

HAMZA: *(Hesitates)* Hamza.

(HAMZA shakes KEVIN's hand.)

KEVIN: You keep practicing.

HAMZA: I will.

KEVIN: Don't let your parents discourage you.

HAMZA: They don't.

KEVIN: I hear a musician struggling to get out.

HAMZA: Yeah, well, we'll see.

KEVIN: He's half-way out already.

HAMZA: I hope so.

KEVIN: I know so.... The music isn't far behind either.

(Slight beat. KEVIN *leans forward and tries to kiss* HAMZA. HAMZA *pulls back. A quick beat as* KEVIN *tries to get a reading on* HAMZA.)

KEVIN: Sorry. —I thought...

*(*HAMZA's *manner suggests his pulling back was more surprise than rejection. Kevin leans in to try and kiss him again. Again Hamza pulls back.)*

HAMZA: I can't.

KEVIN: Okay.

HAMZA: I—I can't.

KEVIN: That's fine. No problem. You have a nice day. —I thought—.

HAMZA: No.

KEVIN: Okay. Most times. This area... You didn't know?

HAMZA: It's not a good idea.

KEVIN: What isn't? —Why not? We're safe. Nothing unsafe will happen...I like you.

HAMZA: I don't do that. I don't.... I don't do that.

KEVIN: What?

HAMZA: This?

KEVIN: What this?

HAMZA: I can't.

KEVIN: You keep saying that, but you're not leaving.... Not that you have to. You don't have to budge an inch. There's enough room in whatever you're feeling to—to relax.

HAMZA: *(More excuse than explanation)* I'm fasting.

KEVIN: *(A laugh)* What?

HAMZA: I'm—fasting. I can't do this.

KEVIN: Oh. Right. Fasting. What's it called? I know that. Until the sun goes down, right. "Ramadan." *(Looks towards the sunset)* It's almost down.

(The lights are indeed changing and have been changing throughout the scene.)

HAMZA: I have to go home.

KEVIN: Is it a high? Fasting? I'd love to try it one day. I find so much of that culture intriguing. I wish I was a Muslim.

HAMZA: Why?

KEVIN: I don't know. I just think I'd take to it.

HAMZA: Muslims don't do this.

KEVIN: Sure they do. One of my best lovers was a Muslim.

HAMZA: He wasn't a real Muslim then.

KEVIN: He thought he was. Is that what's troubling you? Not what a devout Muslim does? Is a devout Muslim and a devout human being two different things? It's a shame how so many religions end up being such killjoys.

HAMZA: My religion isn't that.

KEVIN: I can relate. I was a Catholic. I loved the whole thing. Loved the saints, loved praying to Mary. I just couldn't take being called a perpetual sinner.

HAMZA: You don't believe in God?

KEVIN: Sure I do. After that I joined the Pentecostals. Something about speaking in tongues and handling snakes appealed to my lawyer nature. —I'm kidding. Don't be scared. Nothing is going to happen if you don't want it to.

HAMZA: So you don't believe in God?

KEVIN: I do. Very much so.

HAMZA: How can you be doing this then?

KEVIN: Because in my universe God is gay. What, you think he's straight? Isn't that just as dumb as thinking God is gay? I don't think he gives a damn. I don't think he has sex. I don't think he's as sex-obsessed as the people who speak on his behalf are.

HAMZA: I need to get home.

KEVIN: What really pisses me off is how religion screws people like you up. Don't waste these years like I almost did. Never mind what's *not* going to happen between us. Nothing will. But don't...don't get all twisted up inside about it.

HAMZA: About what? Nothing's happened. I don't know what you're talking about.

(Slight beat)

KEVIN: Okay... Whatever. —It's your life. But just... *(Slight beat)* What if it's not a flaw. That you have to struggle against. What if it's a way for you to open up to the world. A blessing. A blessing even... Think about that.

HAMZA: *(Slight beat)* You're a lawyer. They make arguments. Not music.

KEVIN: That's right.... And I wasn't just flattering you about being good. Keep playing. *(Slight beat)* And— maybe I'll see you around.

(HAMZA doesn't move. KEVIN turns to look at the last light.)

KEVIN: The sun's going down.

(A park light goes on, throwing a spot on HAMZA and KEVIN.)

KEVIN: Just in time. You're on. Your very own spotlight. It's calling out for one last tune. *(Slight*

beat) Go on…. Play something. *(Slight beat)* Play me
something.

(Beat. Blackout)

Scene 7

*(Living room. The room is empty. We hear the sound of
a sewing machine. The front door is heard opening and
shutting off-stage.)*

KAMAL: *(Off-stage)* Huwaida? …Hamza? *(He appears
at the doorway carrying a soup container in a plastic bag.)*
Where's the furniture? Mona? —Where is everyone? —
Mona? *(Then he sees the footprints on the floor. He quickly
slips out of his shoes and walks in.)* Are they doing this on
purpose?

*(MONA appears at another doorway unwinding thread from
u spool.)*

MONA: How's Aziz?

KAMAL: *(Pointing to the floor)* What is that?

MONA: It's the jinn, my love. They're coming out to
celebrate the engagement. They've been dancing.
Dancing and jumping and having a good time, as we
should.

KAMAL: Jinn don't wear sneakers.

MONA: Come on, let's dance.

(MONA moves towards KAMAL and takes him in her arms.)

KAMAL: *(Breaking away from her)* It's as if my word
means nothing anymore. And where's the furniture?
It's "iftar" already.

MONA: *(Looking at her watch)* So it is. I forgot the time.
I'll go heat the food. *(She starts to exit into the kitchen.)*

KAMAL: Where are they? And where are we going to eat? They said they'd put the furniture back.

MONA: We'll do it after dinner. We'll bring out the table for now.

KAMAL: On this? *(Pointing to the floor)* I'm not cleaning this up.

MONA: *(Stopping at the doorway)* Don't. I think we should draw a chalk out-line around the dirt as evidence.

(The front door shuts off-stage rather loudly.)

KAMAL: This has become the sound of our children.

MONA: Tawfiq?

(HUWAIDA comes in taking her veil off. She drops her backpack. KAMAL puts his hand out for her to stop. HUWAIDA stops)

MONA: Help your father roll the carpets out and clean that up, please. And I want to measure the sleeves again. *(She exits, off-stage)* And bring out the table.

HUWAIDA: *(Slipping out of her shoes)* Why hasn't the furniture been put back?

KAMAL: You and your brothers were supposed to do it.

HUWAIDA: They said they'd take care of it.

KAMAL: Well they didn't. *(Reining in his irritation)* Never mind. You have special exemption. How are you?

HUWAIDA: I'm—okay. *(She takes the mop from the corner.)*

KAMAL: That's all. Aren't you excited?

HUWAIDA: About what?

KAMAL: "About what?", she says. Is this how the next generation views marriage? The next big step in your life is just another day?

HUWAIDA: Where's the dirt?

(KAMAL *hugs her.*)

KAMAL: "Habibti." My darling girl. Look at you now.
Look how far you've come. You could've turned out
so many different ways, but here you are: a jewel. A
wonderful daughter.

HUWAIDA: I can't breathe.

KAMAL: Don't move to a different state.

HUWAIDA: It's an engagement not a marriage.

KAMAL: I am so proud of you.

HUWAIDA: If you squeeze any harder I'm going to faint.

(MONA *enters carrying two sleeves of a dress, one of them
draped across her shoulder. Kamal eases up on his hug but
continues to hold* HUWAIDA.)

KAMAL: (*To* MONA, *about* HUWAIDA) Look at her. Look
at this woman. When did she become a woman?

HUWAIDA: Can I clean this up so we can eat?

(MONA *measures the sleeves out against each of*
HUWAIDA's *arms, marking it with chalk; doing so even
when* HUWAIDA *starts cleaning. Perhaps, also, she has a
measuring tape, which she might proceed to use.*)

KAMAL: We have a woman for a daughter. Full grown.
Able to walk. And go to university and get married.
Yesterday we were wiping your ka-ka, tomorrow you
might run for Congress.

HUWAIDA: (*Sarcastic*) Right. Why not run for President.

KAMAL: You can. You were born here. You have the
right. (*To* MONA) Think of that. Our children can
become Presidents.

HUWAIDA: The first veiled President of the United
States. That I'd like to see.

KAMAL: Why not? They've elected a lot stranger.

MONA: Hold still.

KAMAL: Everything is possible.

MONA: *(To* KAMAL*)* Is Aziz well enough to come?

KAMAL: He'll be here. It was just jet lag. What a
wonderful boy Murad is. He's grown up to be a real
man.

HUWAIDA: So I hear.

KAMAL: As nice in person as he is over the phone.

MONA: And if you don't like him, we can call it off.

KAMAL: Of course, of course. You are not committed to
anything yet. Nothing has been signed and no prayers
uttered. You are free to walk away. Like everyone else
does in this country when they're not in the mood
anymore. When it upsets their precious little freedoms.

MONA: *(To* KAMAL*)* Why don't you get the carpets out.

KAMAL: Did you hear about your brother? He has
made a great discovery: there is no God.

HUWAIDA: I heard.

KAMAL: *(To* MONA*)* You must remind me to ask him
for his proof of this.

MONA: *(To* HUWAIDA*)* Go bring in the small carpet.

*(*HUWAIDA *gives her mother the mop and exits.* KAMAL
continues talking.)

KAMAL: It's a pity he didn't discover this in high
school, he could've made it his science project.

MONA: Kamal.

*(*MONA *goes to another exit and deposits the mop off-stage.)*

KAMAL: I wanted to bring it up with Aziz; to warn him,
just in case. His father was a sheikh in Al-Azhar; he
might take offense. I wanted to make a joke of it and

say see how crazy this country can make you. But I couldn't. I couldn't laugh about it. I find no place in my heart for this thing to settle.

MONA: And if tomorrow I said I was an atheist, would it change anything? Would it make a difference in our relationship?

KAMAL: Yes. I would seek medical advice. I'd be worried this was a sign of menopause, or you were losing your mind.

MONA: And I would seek a divorce because you were acting so stupid.

KAMAL: Mona—be careful. I have only so much humor today and I am very upset.

MONA: It's not about you, Kamal.

KAMAL: It's about *us*—our family. The ground upon which we raised our children and everything else that has kept us together.

MONA: He's a grown man; he's free to believe what he wants.

(HUWAIDA *enters dragging in a carpet.* MONA *goes to help her. Followed by* KAMAL)

KAMAL: *(To* HUWAIDA*)* Your mother has become an atheist. Say something. Your religion is being challenged.

MONA: *(To* HUWAIDA*)* What's wrong? You look like you're coming down with a cold?

(MONA *places her hand on* HUWAIDA'*s forehead.*)

HUWAIDA: I don't want to get engaged tomorrow.

(*The other two stop what they're doing. Beat*)

HUWAIDA: That was a joke. I wanted to see what your reaction would be.

(*The front door is heard slamming loudly off-stage.*)

HUWAIDA: I'll get the other carpet.

(HUWAIDA *exits.* KAMAL *and* MONA *look at each other.* TAWFIQ *appears in the doorway.*)

KAMAL: Where were you?

TAWFIQ: I'm sorry, I was—I got held up.

KAMAL: You said you would help us.

TAWFIQ: (*Slipping out of his shoes*) I'll do it right now.

KAMAL: Thank you for gracing us with your presence. I understand how difficult it must be to mix with people who have such primitive beliefs.

MONA: Kamal.

KAMAL: Poor God. To have become a figment of our imagination. And us poor savages for building civilizations around this figment.

(TAWFIQ *has crossed the room and exited.*)

MONA: I beg you. Don't push this. Don't drive him away.

KAMAL: I will speak to my son anyway I wish.

MONA: If he leaves, I will leave with him.

KAMAL: Do as you wish. I can book you in the same motel as Aziz right now.

MONA: Can you *please* leave this alone?

KAMAL: No!—It is like a chicken bone stuck in my throat and I will have any conversation I want in my own home!

MONA: Perhaps it is about you after all. You make believing in God such a pain in the ass.

KAMAL: Go get the food ready. And find out what your daughter just said. What kind of joke is that? Is everyone losing their minds?

(MONA *exits into the kitchen. Slight beat*)

KAMAL: This is my house! I will speak anyway I choose!

(HUWAIDA *and* TAWFIQ *enter carrying the big carpet. To* HUWAIDA:)

KAMAL: What was that? You were being funny? What kind of humor is that? Are you getting engaged to this boy or what?

HUWAIDA: Yes.

KAMAL: Then why did you say that?

HUWAIDA: I was just...I didn't mean anything by it.

KAMAL: Huwaida: I am in no mood for jokes. Save that for your brothers. (*To* TAWFIQ) And where is Hamza? Where is he?

TAWFIQ: I don't know.

(KAMAL *is about to launch into something but interrupts himself with:*)

KAMAL: I will tell you both now I have only this much patience for your nonsense. Our house is not a circus for your silly behavior. You will leave that rubbish outside when you come in here. (*Considers going on, instead:*) What is wrong with people today?

(KAMAL *exits.* HUWAIDA *and* TAWFIQ *are unrolling the carpet.*)

TAWFIQ: You *have* changed your mind.

HUWAIDA: I was joking, didn't you hear?

TAWFIQ: You don't want to go through with it.

HUWAIDA: You'd love that wouldn't you.

TAWFIQ: *Tell* them.

HUWAIDA: I don't want to talk to you, Tawfiq.

TAWFIQ: I'll back you up all the way.

HUWAIDA: Thanks, you'd be a great advocate to have.

TAWFIQ: You're going to do it just to please them? To spite me?

HUWAIDA: Oh, get a grip; you have such an inflated sense of yourself.

TAWFIQ: And you're pig-headed enough to go through with it.

(HUWAIDA *gets ready to exit,* TAWFIQ *stops her.)*

TAWFIQ: What happened with Murad? What did he say?

HUWAIDA: *(Facing him)* You were right. He's a hick. He spoke of nothing but love. How backward is that.

(HUWAIDA *exits.* KAMAL *enters carrying two dining room chairs. [If a table can be assembled, perhaps he brings in one half of a table instead of a second chair.]* TAWFIQ *exits.* KAMAL *deposits the furniture and stands there for a moment. Then:)*

KAMAL: This should have been done already! I don't want to assemble the table now!

MONA: *(Off-stage)* Tawfiq. Bring in the coffee table. Never mind the dining room set. Let's eat first. —Did you hear me?

TAWFIQ: *(Off-stage)* Yes!

(KAMAL *sits on the chair, exhausted.* HUWAIDA *enters carrying a chair. She puts it down.)*

KAMAL: *(Calmly, without threat)* You do want this boy, don't you?

HUWAIDA: Yes, Puppy.

KAMAL: I don't want to force him on you. It's the last thing we want to do.

HUWAIDA: It's my decision.

KAMAL: I have no interest in losing you. I would love for my favorite girl to live with me for many more years.

HUWAIDA: I'm not going anywhere. I'll still be here.

(Whether or not he extends his arm for her to come, his manner beckons for her to draw close. She does so. He hugs her, still sitting down.)

KAMAL: I want what will make you happy…. Only that.

*(*TAWFIQ *enters carrying a coffee table.* MONA *enters carrying a large soup bowl, ladle and cutlery.)*

MONA: *(To* TAWFIQ*)* Put it right here.

*(*TAWFIQ *deposits the coffee table where indicated.* MONA *puts down the soup bowl.)*

MONA: Someone bring in the bowls. And the bread. And bring in the fruit.

*(*TAWFIQ *and* MONA *exit into the kitchen.)*

MONA: We can start with the "ats" and bring out the rest later when Hamza comes.

KAMAL: This is not like him.

MONA: It's probably traffic.

KAMAL: Did he tell you he'd be late?

MONA: No. There's a good reason, I'm sure. *(She lays out the cutlery.)*

KAMAL: I apologize if I was…unpleasant…. Even though everything I said was right.

MONA: Of course it was. You'd stop breathing if you were proven wrong.

KAMAL: Can we still get married again tomorrow?

MONA: No. I'd rather not do anything to remind me I am married to you already. You can be horrible, you know that.

KAMAL: No. I can be right in a way that pleases no one. That is not the same thing.

MONA: And the rest of us are stupid?

KAMAL: I didn't say that. I am speaking of things we have all agreed on.

MONA: *(Avoiding an argument)* Let's just eat. Everyone's nerves have had enough.

KAMAL: Where are we going to sit?

MONA: On your precious carpets. *(To off-stage)* Huwaida?

(HUWAIDA enters with plates of bread and fruit. Soon followed by TAWFIQ carrying a pitcher of water and glasses. They will set them on the coffee table.)

MONA: We're going to start.

HUWAIDA: We're not waiting?

MONA: Didn't any of you speak with Hamza?

TAWFIQ: I think he was going to practice his oud.

MONA: Maybe he's breaking his fast elsewhere. I'm sure he's fine.

HUWAIDA: Where are we going to sit?

MONA: Hasn't anyone heard of the floor? We wouldn't have to be sitting on it if you'd come home sooner.

(They stand there for a moment.)

MONA: Are we going to eat or not?

(KAMAL descends from his chair to the coffee table. The others, each in turn, sit down around the table. MONA starts pouring water into the glasses. They all sit there for a moment. Perhaps KAMAL looks towards the door.)

KAMAL: This is not like him.... He would've called.

HUWAIDA: Maybe he finally figured out how to play and lost track of the time.

MONA: Let's just start.

(KAMAL raises his palms in prayer. Slight beat.)

KAMAL: *En el nombre de Allah, El Clemente, El Misercordioso*... And that's all I know in Spanish.

HUWAIDA: Where did you learn that?

KAMAL: Luis. He invited us for "iftar" next week.

(KAMAL drinks. HUWAIDA passes a bowl to MONA to start ladling the "ats".)

TAWFIQ: *(To his mother)* I can do that.

(TAWFIQ takes the ladle from MONA. HUWAIDA will pass the bowls to her brother. MONA passes the bread around.)

KAMAL: He promised us tamales if we come. Rice with frijoles. And those fried banana things. *(To MONA)* I have a special request. Would it be too much if we skipped "ats" for one day. As lovely as you make them, I'd be happy if I never saw lentils again for the rest of Ramadan. Anything that does not look like a bean would be appreciated.

TAWFIQ: Let us thank God and be grateful for the bounty he provides.

(The two women tense up in anticipation of KAMAL's reaction. KAMAL looks at TAWFIQ.)

KAMAL: What?

TAWFIQ: *(Continuing to ladle; hesitates)* Let's be thankful for...for what we have.

KAMAL: *(Slight beat)* Are you being funny with us?

TAWFIQ: No. I was—

KAMAL: Are you being sarcastic with me?

TAWFIQ: No, I'm just saying, let's be thankful for what we—

KAMAL: What is the word "God" doing in your mouth if you don't believe in Him?

TAWFIQ: It's a...it's an expression.

KAMAL: An expression? —Are you mocking us?

MONA: Kamal.

KAMAL: Are you spitting our religion back in our face? What are you even doing here if you're not fasting anymore.

TAWFIQ: I *am* fasting.

KAMAL: Why? If not to remember God for what reason?

TAWFIQ: To keep you company.

KAMAL: Thank you, we'll do without. It is no company to have someone who mocks us sitting at our table.

MONA: *Please.* Let us eat and have this discussion later. We need to put *something* in our stomachs before we say another word.

(Silence. KAMAL fumes. People hesitantly begin to eat. Then:)

KAMAL: "An expression."

TAWFIQ: I was trying to say we should be grateful for whatever mother cooks for us.

(KAMAL slams his bowl or spoon down.)

KAMAL: Get out!

TAWFIQ: Why?

MONA: Stop it!

KAMAL: Get out!

TAWFIQ: I was just saying we have no reason to complain.

KAMAL: Are you now telling me how I should speak to my wife?

TAWFIQ: *No.*

MONA: Kamal!

(The telephone rings off-stage. To TAWFIQ*:)*

MONA: Go see who it is. It's probably Hamza.

*(*TAWFIQ *rises and exits. Slight beat. Then:)*

HUWAIDA: Mommy. Puppy. There's probably not a good time to tell you this. And I am actually not one hundred per cent sure if I should—tell you; or, if I didn't—whether I should go ahead any way because I'm not, as I said, certain. —And I guess you're not in the mood to hear this now, but...what I said earlier—was probably accurate. And while it's possible I was joking when I said it to hear how it sounded, I was most likely telling the truth. About not wanting to get engaged. I think—in thinking about it—I was telling the truth. *(Slight beat)* That's...that's basically it.

MONA: I didn't understand a word you said.

*(*TAWFIQ *enters.)*

TAWFIQ: It's Hamza. —He's calling from—from jail. He's...he's in jail. —He's been arrested.

(Beat. Blackout. Intermission)

END OF ACT ONE

ACT TWO

Scene 1

(Spotlight on PAULINE. *Her speech is addressed out to the audience.)*

PAULINE: Huwaida…I know I may be overstepping a line…but I feel…I do feel I need to say something. Not as a therapist—but as another person struggling to figure things out, like you. I feel now it would be wrong if I didn't. You wanted something definitive from me, something concrete, so…here it is. You were right…I do have a question about your veiling. —I do think the dream was speaking directly to it. It couldn't be any clearer to my mind. And I know you insist it shouldn't be reduced to that; and that it isn't about "liberating you from the veil" but, Huwaida—how liberating is something that prevents you from even questioning it? Which I think you're doing, and are feeling distressed because you're not giving yourself permission to do so. And I can't imagine that's what any religion is supposed to do. Protect, yes, but imprison? —I am trying to be sensitive to your faith and I know I'm woefully ignorant and God knows we could all do a little more to jump these abysses that separate us but, I do think…I just…I have to come right out and say that I think your religion is bad news for women. And I'm not sure it's right to be "culturally sensitive" when a system perpetuates injustices. And yes: I've heard how Islam was a great liberator of women and gave them rights that we in the West only began to get in the 19th century, but we're not living back then, and from what I've seen, if that is true, your religion has stopped being a living, breathing support and has become instead an excuse for men to put down women. And yes we could get into a history lesson about how all religions have done that, but again we're not talking about that. You're making your life now, in America, and I honestly don't know if the two go well together. I'm sorry for being so blunt. But it was only after you left that I realized how offended I was by what your wearing of that veil meant to me. And the degree to which you'd been brainwashed into believing that was okay. It's not. It's not okay when we buy into our own oppressions. It's not okay that we take on the prejudices of one gender and make them our own. So that we women end up being the gatekeepers of our own oppression; to the point that we make of our manacles things of pride and even become vain about it. I don't know how you can call yourself a feminist and say that, and cover yourself as if you have something to be ashamed about, as if you have *anything* to apologize for.

(HUWAIDA *enters. Lights up on the area where the two interact. She has had a complete makeover. She wears a revealing, "sexy" dress. Just shy of being gaudy, and clearly meant to be provocative. Or it could be a tank top and short skirt. Again, not quite over-the-top, but obviously meant to turn heads. Also, she wears make-up. And her hair has been brushed out.*)

HUWAIDA: How about now? ...How do I look? — Liberated? —Am I more pleasing to you? Am I the picture of mental health now? Is this what you're recommending?

PAULINE: Huwaida.

HUWAIDA: Too much? Less blush? Are my breasts showing too much? How would you have me?

PAULINE: This is not what I meant.

HUWAIDA: You obviously have a standard in mind, what is it? Is my lipstick too red?

PAULINE: It's not about any of that.

HUWAIDA: Yes it is, dress me. Unshackle me from my manacles. Help me be a better feminist. Or am I not a feminist wearing this? Should I let my underarm hair grow? Is that it? Let it all hang out. Burn my bra. Put a little jiggle in my breasts as I march down the street declaring my womanhood. Is that the standard?

PAULINE: I'm talking about your emotional life. What we carry inside and how that expresses itself, either as a support or hindrance.

HUWAIDA: *(Referring to what she's wearing)* And what does this express? Freedom? The road to success as a woman?

PAULINE: I never said that.

HUWAIDA: Yes you did. If not the veil then this. Variations of this.

PAULINE: There are as many ways to dress as there are individuals.

HUWAIDA: Except it's funny how we all look the same from one fashion cycle to another. Gee, you might even call it a uniform.

PAULINE: Look, I understand the point you're making.—

HUWAIDA: *(Interrupting)* Is this not in fashion this season? Should I be mortified that I have no sense of "what's in" and waste a whole life jumping through *those* hoops.

PAULINE: I agree: we're always conforming to one standard or another, and they can be just as oppressive—

HUWAIDA: *(Interrupting)* Yes they can, so why not choose one based on the spirit and not on the meat market?

PAULINE: Because I don't see any signs of God in demanding women hide themselves. It seems to be the flip-side of the meat market, seeing women as nothing but provocative creatures that have to be hidden away for everyone's protection. Which doesn't mean you have to jump to this. *(Referring to what HUWAIDA's wearing)*

HUWAIDA: What are you, the fashion police? Going around telling people what is and isn't appropriate? And what is your problem that you can't get beyond a frickin' headscarf? I come to you carrying a wealth of faith and you want to *cure* me of that?

PAULINE: Are you saying that Muslim women who don't wear the veil are any less religious?

HUWAIDA: It's how *I* choose to express it. Your receptionist is wearing a thumping big cross the size of her blouse, why is that alright? Why isn't she harassed or called brainwashed?

PAULINE: It doesn't prevent her from doing what she wants.

HUWAIDA: *Because it's accepted. She's not harassed about it and made to feel like a freak.*

PAULINE: Then perhaps you're experiencing the veil as a burden.

HUWAIDA: I never said that!

PAULINE: I think your dream did.

HUWAIDA: Oh screw my dream, that's your interpretation. I wish I'd never told you about it.

(Slight beat)

PAULINE: And yet here you are...you came back.

HUWAIDA: I came back because I was pissed off by what you said. I wanted to come back wearing the conclusion that everything you said implied. I don't know what it is about women professors here that they feel impelled to save us. As if we needed your precious help when you spend most of your life agonizing over the dumbest, f'd-up things. Go crusade someone else's ass.

PAULINE: Did you come back just to tell me this?

HUWAIDA: You're not listening, are you.

PAULINE: I am. Very closely.

HUWAIDA: Then I guess your English is not the same as mine

(She starts to leave but stops when Pauline talks.)

PAULINE: My door is always open.

HUWAIDA: No. It's not. It hasn't opened once.

(Blackout. In the blackout, we hear the sound of an airplane taking off.)

Scene 2

(Lights up on a neutral area. Though it's MURAD's motel room, it's also his dreamscape. So it could also incorporate HUWAIDA's family living room, if that's simpler in terms of set transitions. He is asleep in a chair or on a couch.)

(Standing next to MURAD is H D She is wearing a hijab and a long flowing dress, her face showing. The effect is elegant and neat.)

(We hear the "ping" sound heard on airplanes.)

PILOT: *(Over the speakers)* Crosscheck.

(MURAD sits up. He sees H D And is startled.)

H D: Hi. I'm Huwaida's double. "H D" for short. You're welcome to call me that, all my friends do. And I have a feeling we're going to be fast friends.

MURAD: Where...

H D: Where are you?

MURAD: Yes.

H D: Well, wouldn't you know, we're in a dream. Yours. And I thank you for hosting it as I needed a break from Huwaida. She's getting a little too frazzled for me, and though I am part of her unconscious and therefore responsible for helping her act out her issues, there's only so much chaos I can stand before I need the fresh air of someone else's dream-life.

MURAD: You...don't look anything like Huwaida.

H D: I know. There are some benefits to living in the dream world.

MURAD: I'm... *(Looking around, dazed)* I'm rather fond of the way she looks.

H D: Are you? I thought you might be. I caught that gleam in your eye when you were looking at her.

MURAD: *(Looks at his watch)* I have a flight to catch. I'm late.

(MURAD stands up. The sound of the airplane "ping" is heard)

PILOT: *(Over the speakers)* Crosscheck.

H D: Actually that's what I wanted to talk to you about.

(MURAD starts looking around for his suitcase.)

MURAD: Where are my things?

H D: I think all in all it would be best if you didn't go.

MURAD: Where are all my clothes?

H D: If I could have your attention.

MURAD: She said "no" or haven't you heard?

H D: "No", "yes", when you're confused they could mean the same thing.

MURAD: I have to go. Where's my suitcase?

PILOT: *(Over the speakers)* You are now free to walk around the cabin.

H D: Murad, listen to me. It's a universal law of physics that you can't change directions in mid-jump. You'll spend the rest of your life wondering what might have happened. Finish the jump and then make your decision.

MURAD: I am finished, I'm going home.

H D: That's not the direction you took. You're leaping against the current.

MURAD: What concern is my business to you?

H D: Because Huwaida's jumping right there with you and if she falls she's going to crash in on *my* head and right on through to parts of herself that even *I* don't go into. And I will not have her low self-esteem demons messing me up when I'm this close to winning the pageant.

MURAD: What pageant?

PILOT: *(Over the speakers)* We strongly recommend you keep your voices down as we need to hear the engines to fly this plane.

H D: *(Referring to the pilot)* Okay, Murad. You need to take that out. I'm not competing with your unconscious. While I'm here, you need to clear the deck.

(A lunch-box is slid out of the wings. MURAD *and* H D *see it.)*

MURAD: Is that—? That can't be my suitcase.

(A CUSTOMS OFFICER *enters.)*

CUSTOMS OFFICER: *(To* H D*)* Is that your suitcase?

H D: Oh for godsakes.

CUSTOMS OFFICER: *(To* MURAD*)* Is that your suitcase?

H D: *(To* MURAD*)* Make him go away.

MURAD: *(To* H D*)* Please go away.

CUSTOMS OFFICER: Whose suitcase is this?

MURAD: I didn't come with that.

CUSTOMS OFFICER: Uh-huh. *(Into a walkie-talkie)* Bomb squad.

H D: Murad!

CUSTOMS OFFICER: *(To* MURAD*)* Passport please.

*(*MURAD *searches his pockets for his passport.)*

H D: *(To* MURAD*)* You don't need a passport. This is your dream, you can travel anywhere you want.

MURAD: This is not my country; I don't belong here.

H D: Yes you do. You and this place are a perfect fit.

CUSTOMS OFFICER: *(To* MURAD*)* I need to see your passport.

H D: *(To* MURAD*)* You can always go back if it doesn't work out.

CUSTOMS OFFICER: Passport.

H D: *(To* CUSTOMS OFFICER*)* Shut up.

CUSTOMS OFFICER: *(To* H D*)* Yours as well, lady.

H D: *(Giving him the finger)* Stamp this, asshole.

(Three people in bomb-squad clothes enter. Their heads/faces are covered with head gear and dark visors that mask their faces.)

(The CUSTOMS OFFICER *backs up, suddenly wary of the potential danger.* MURAD's *attention turns to the lunch-box. He starts approaching it. As does the bomb squad, staying a few steps behind him.)*

MURAD: *(To* H D*)* You must go now. —Just go. Coming here…expecting things to magically work out, this was the crazy part. Neither of us were thinking.

H D: I wouldn't be here if you didn't secretly know something was up. I have no idea if you can work things out or if you two can live together. But your coming now was no arrangement. Your parents didn't force this on you. Your dream-lives have been working this out for years.

*(*MURAD, *now kneeling in front of the lunch-box, opens it. The bomb squad gasps in fear. He takes out a photo)*

H D: There! You see: it's Huwaida. What does that tell you?

BOMB EXPERT 1: False alarm.

MURAD: She canceled the engagement.

H D: She still has to get used to you. The real you, in the flesh.

BOMB EXPERT 2: Wait! Maybe the photo is wired to explode.

BOMB EXPERT 1: Oh God.

H D: *(To the bomb squad)* Get a grip.

BOMB EXPERT 3: They're hiding explosives everywhere now.

BOMB EXPERT 1: Look at the smile, isn't that a trigger?

BOMB EXPERT 2: It's in the smile!

BOMB EXPERT 3: The whole goddamn face is wired.

BOMB EXPERT 2: Grab the photo!

(They push MURAD *aside and grab the photo. Perhaps they put it in a special container as they run and exit.)*

(As they exit:)

BOMB EXPERT 3: Duck! Duck! Get the disposal ready!

MURAD: I'd never survive in America.

H D: It's a little whacky, yes, but that's what's so lovable about it.

MURAD: *(Getting up)* I don't want to live my life as a foreigner. I don't want to have that eating away at me. I can be of more value in my country.

H D: Fine. Run from your future. But I'm telling you this decision will bug you for the rest of your life.

*(*MURAD *takes a few steps in one direction.)*

H D: Egypt's that way, if you're leaving. *(Extends her hand)* Here. I'll take you. I swear to you you'll regret this. Ready?

*(*MURAD *takes* H D's *hand. The sound of the airplane "ping")*

PILOT: *(Over the speakers)* Crosscheck.

*(*H D *and* MURAD *take a step forward. Lights change to something more mellow and peaceful. He lets go of her hand and walks around as if on familiar ground.)*

H D: Happy now? —Don't let this mellow peaceful lighting fool you. It's just your memory doing a makeover.

MURAD: I would miss the skies over my city.

H D: What are you talking about? You can hardly see anything through the pollution.

MURAD: I would miss the streets. The broken pavements. The mess.

H D: You almost got killed crossing the road, remember?

MURAD: The faces. The look of the people. Knowing what gestures mean.

H D: People are strange and familiar everywhere. Even family members can become strangers to us sometimes.

MURAD: I would miss the language.

H D: Would you stop with these excuses before you bury yourself in them!

MURAD: I would miss the call to prayer most of all.

(The call to prayer is heard playing very faintly in the background)

MURAD: Hearing that in the morning. Waking up to it. The whole day waking up to those sounds. Like your whole family has come in to kiss you good-morning. Calling on the best in you to meet the day…yes…I would miss that most of all.

H D: You would carry that always. In your heart. But yours…you will lose yours if you're not careful.

MURAD: Who are you to judge me?

H D: Perhaps I am also calling on the best in you. I am not as beautiful as the call to prayer, but I am a call just the same. From a place messier and just as important. And if God is everywhere, might He not be in that place too and speak to us in many ways, and guises? In impulses, and crazy whims that might just turn out to be right? Why shut yourself off from that? You love mystery too much to do that…. I can't promise you things will work out; no one can. But I do know you started something and you can't live like you didn't. Finish the jump. Fall if you have to, but finish it.

(H D *extends out her hand. Slight beat*)

MURAD: In dreams, when you fall from a great height, doesn't it hurt there as well? Might it not even kill you?

H D: Only if you don't wake up.

(Slight beat. H D's arm remains extended. Blackout)

Scene 3

(Family living room. Most of the furniture has been brought in. The furniture is at odd angles and positions, still waiting to be put in its proper place. The oud is on the coffee table.)

(KAMAL stands. MONA sits on a chair. HAMZA is also seated, staring fixedly ahead.)

(Silence)

(TAWFIQ enters dragging in two more pieces of furniture. He pauses for a couple of beats, unsure of what to do next. He moves one of the pieces to its proper place. Then drags the coffee table a few feet to where it's supposed to be—which happens to be beside KAMAL. KAMAL looks at the oud.)

TAWFIQ: *(To MONA)* Want me to assemble the table now?

MONA: *(Slight beat)* What?

HAMZA: Can I go to my room, please?

KAMAL: No.

(KAMAL picks up the oud. Beat)

MONA: We should rest. We've been up too long. —We can speak about this later.

(Slight beat. TAWFIQ hesitantly sits next to HAMZA. Perhaps he reaches out to touch his hand. HAMZA stands abruptly and moves away. KAMAL plucks on the oud.)

KAMAL: *(To* HAMZA, *but not directly)* Did you even
practice? *(Strumming a few strings)* My mother always
thought it a vice of my father's, playing this.... He
would come home and get drunk on this instrument....
Shut us out with the pleasure he found in it....
Sometimes making us be his audience.... We would
dutifully listen...and sometimes enjoy. But most
times...I would grit my teeth...and pray the song was
short.... He made it seem such a joy...I envied him his
passion.... I always wondered where he went in his
head when he played.

MONA: "Allah yirhamou." He was a good man.

KAMAL: Yes.... Perhaps it is best he is dead after
all.... He would have been upset that the grandson
who continued his passion was caught with a man in
the bushes. And that his beautiful oud was nearby.
"What," he would have said, "you couldn't have left
the oud behind? You had to drag it into your filthy
habit?"

*(*HAMZA *exits the room.* KAMAL *shouts after him.)*

KAMAL: "This, an inspired instrument, that calls out
the best in us, this you had to have next to you while
you were debasing yourself?"

MONA: I knew you could handle this properly. I was
worried the wisdom of Solomon might be absent in
this time when we need it most.

KAMAL: This will be in his record. This—stain. This...
abomination. This is public record. You know this is
public record? For everyone to see. This will spread
like wild fire—in the community, and back to Egypt.
Oh they will love this. We will be the best show in
town. We are supplying them with all the drama they
need. Switch off your televisions and come see the
Fawzi family as they explode. First my son goes insane
and becomes an atheist. Then my daughter goes insane

and dumps the engagement. And now my other son
goes insane and goes fornicating in the bushes. What
happened? Did they change the drinking water on
us? Is there a virus going round that is effecting our
ability to be sane? Decent? Oh: *(A short laugh)* we did
a wonderful job. You especially my dear, with your
wonderful skill of cursing your children with all the
freedom they could ever want.

MONA: Enough.

KAMAL: Not enough. What's next? Suddenly I find
myself in a new family with new rules and thinking.
What is up next? Let it *all* happen. Bring it all on today.

TAWFIQ: You know—I just don't think we need to make
a big deal about this. I really don't.

KAMAL: Yes! Listen to our son. He has the solution. Of
course he has. We, pitiful we, who were not born of
this soil are behind the times. How could we not accept
the right to fuck in the street.

MONA: Please stop with this language.

KAMAL: The *language* upsets you? After what's
happened, this is what upsets you?

TAWFIQ: So what?

KAMAL: "So what?" Your solution is this?

TAWFIQ: No one was harmed. This isn't a crime.

KAMAL: Tell me: in your world, what is a big deal?
Perhaps I missed something important growing up and
need to go back to school.

*(Agitated, MONA starts arranging the furniture, dragging
pieces here and there. Kamal continues:)*

KAMAL: Okay, let me understand this: so, logically,
according to you, for instance, since they tell us to
be kind and treat animals nicely, when humans start
behaving like animals and have sex in public, I should

call the S P C A for guidance? I should call an animal rights group for moral guidance? Yes, yes, how could I have been so stupid and intolerant. Invite them here. Let them meet the sheikh and the imam so we can all discuss God, dogs and fucking in public.

TAWFIQ: Puppy:—

KAMAL: *(Interrupting)* Would this be tolerant enough for you?

TAWFIQ: He's—. Hamza's—…

KAMAL: "La'a." Don't say it.

TAWFIQ: Yes he is.

KAMAL: "Harram." Don't drag them into this. Even they would be offended.

TAWFIQ: But, that's—that what he is, he's—.

KAMAL: My son is not that! *(To MONA)* And if you say "so what," I swear to God—

MONA: *(Interrupting, forceful, stopping what she's doing)* Swear to God what?

TAWFIQ: What were the cops doing prowling around there anyway? Like they don't have more important things to do. That's what ticks me off. Get pissed off with them.

KAMAL: It's their job! It's against the law!

TAWFIQ: Then it should be struck off the books. It's nobody's affair.

KAMAL: There is another book and another law, and these you can not strike out. We apologize we are so ignorant for believing these things.

TAWFIQ: Exactly, that's why he couldn't bring him home.

KAMAL: It's not about where they could do this, it's filthy business wherever they do it!

TAWFIQ: Says who?

KAMAL: Every faith on the planet. Are they all wrong? Was every faith inspired by ignorance that they should come to the same conclusion?

TAWFIQ: Yes, they all came to be at a time when people were weirded out by sex. We've changed. And why on earth would God forbid consenting love between two people?

KAMAL: You call what happened "love"? That is love to you?

TAWFIQ: Why not, it might've been. It might've led to it.

KAMAL: *(To* MONA*)* Listen to your son talk. Two people in the bushes is love to him. This is what it means to live without God. These are the conclusions you come to.

TAWFIQ: I'd rather live without God and have some compassion than have God and use him to punish anything I don't like.

KAMAL: *(Close to* TAWFIQ*)* You don't think I have compassion for my son? *(Even more intense)* You don't think I care for my son? That I would give up my life for him in a second?

TAWFIQ: I'm just saying we shouldn't—

KAMAL: *(Interrupting)* "Compassion"?

MONA: *(Trying to defuse the situation)* Tawfiq. Go and get the rest of the furniture.

KAMAL: Today I went and got my son out of jail and your solution is "so what"?

TAWFIQ: Was he supposed to bring him home and introduce him?

KAMAL: *(Cutting him off firmly)* I don't want to hear another word. *(Slight beat)* Your thinking offers nothing but chaos to do anything you want. No family could survive for a day with your ideas. There is a reason this book and our beliefs have lasted through wars, famine and even America. And yes, it will outlast even you too.

TAWFIQ: And you wonder why I became an atheist.

*(*HAMZA *enters. Everyone stops to look at him. He hesitates a beat.)*

HAMZA: I...I promise you...what happened...it will never happen again. I don't know what...I wasn't... it was never supposed to happen. I wasn't even supposed to be there. I was heading somewhere else. I wanted to...I was going to surprise you with this song. I wanted to practice. I don't know how I...I was just going to practice. I found this quiet place, and he... showed up. And...talked about the oud and knew about it, and I listened. I was coming home; I told him I had to get home but he.... He wanted me to continue. So I played. I played another song. Whatever you think, I'm not—it's not. It's not me. Please don't think that. I'm not...

TAWFIQ: Hamza.

HAMZA: The thought disgusts me. That you would think that of me.

TAWFIQ: You don't have to do this.

HAMZA: It disgusts me. And nothing happened; whatever the police said. I would never do that to you or myself.

TAWFIQ: *(Approaching him)* Don't do this.

HAMZA: *(To* TAWFIQ, *stepping away)* Leave me alone.

TAWFIQ: Don't make it worse.

HAMZA: Leave me alone! *(To* KAMAL *and* MONA*)* It will be alright. I will make it up to you. I promise you.

*(*HAMZA *stands there for a short, awkward beat, then exits. The others stand there for a moment, then:)*

TAWFIQ: Well that was healthy. —Hamza is well on his way to becoming a healthy, functioning member of this society. A few more twists like that and he'll be just screwed-up enough to fit right in.

*(*TAWFIQ *leaves through the same exit as* HAMZA *did.)*

(Silence. Even after the shuffling, the furniture still looks scattered, disordered.)

KAMAL: *(With some exhaustion)* You don't say anything. *(Beat)* Why don't you say anything?

MONA: What do you want me to say? ...You had enough to say without me.

KAMAL: *(Quiet)* One of these days we have to talk about how I have to do all the dirty work...say what needs to be said...and you get to sit there like a saint. And I get to be the bad guy.

MONA: Nobody's calling you that.

KAMAL: One of my sons thinks that.

MONA: He's protective of Hamza.

KAMAL: And I'm not? *(Slight beat)* Did we upset anyone? ...Make someone jealous? That they would give us the evil eye? Really. What did we do wrong? To have the world turn upside down on us? ...Mona, say something. And please don't say they're growing up.

MONA: I just hope he used a condom.

(This is too much for KAMAL. *Perhaps he stands.)*

KAMAL: Thank you. I knew you would say the one thing that would make me feel better.

MONA: We'd better pray he used one. Gay, not gay, we have to make sure.

KAMAL: Thank God the engagement is off. Thank God. Things work out after all. Imagine. "Excuse the mess, we were up all night and morning trying to get our son out of jail for doing something very bad in public and now we're having a discussion about what he should put on his privates."

MONA: What are you protective of? Your son, or your reputation?

KAMAL: I'm protecting him from himself! —To stop him going down a road he doesn't have to go down and make his life a hundred times more difficult.

MONA: Maybe it was a one time thing…. It's possible. You lose your head. We all lose our heads at least once. He had the bad luck to get caught, or the good luck. Now he's embarrassed. He's very ashamed, and he won't ever do it again…. That is also possible.

(Slight beat)

KAMAL: You think so? *(Slight beat)* You really think that?

MONA: *(Slight beat)* I don't know. *(Slight beat)* I don't know anything anymore.

(KAMAL picks up the oud. Inspects it. Turns it over. Then raises it above his head ready to smash it against a piece of furniture.)

MONA: No!

(The doorbell rings. KAMAL freezes. Slight beat)

KAMAL: *(Lowers the oud)* Who's that?

MONA: I called everyone to cancel the engagement party.

KAMAL: Did Huwaida forget her key?

MONA: It might be the Jehovah's Witnesses. I saw them around yesterday.

KAMAL: Wonderful. Tell them to come in. Tell them we're ready to convert.

MONA: Who else could it be?

KAMAL: Tawfiq should open the door. They'll regret ever having come to this house.

(The doorbell rings again. Neither KAMAL nor MONA moves.)

MONA: We're acting like we're hiding out. See who it is.

(KAMAL starts for the exit, handing MONA the oud on his way out. She stands—or sits down. Her manner suggesting something we hadn't seen previously when the others were around: a certain heaviness; the burden of what's occurred.)

AZIZ: *(Accent; off-stage)* "Salaam 'alaykum." "Ahlan, ahlan." *(We hear the sound of kissing on the cheeks)* At last: I get to visit you.

KAMAL: *(Off-stage)* Aziz. This is—. "Fadal." Come in.

(At the sound of his name, MONA is suddenly alert. If she's been sitting, she stands, and looks around at the mess.)

KAMAL: We were just coming to see you.

(AZIZ and KAMAL enter. AZIZ walks with a cane. He carries a wrapped gift of food.)

AZIZ: I said I had to come and say hello. And goodbye. *(To MONA)* Hello.

(MONA goes up to AZIZ.)

MONA: Aziz. Welcome. I'm sorry we didn't come earlier.

(MONA and AZIZ kiss on the cheeks.)

MONA: We were planning to.

AZIZ: No problem.

(AZIZ *hands* MONA *the present.*)

MONA: Thank you.

KAMAL: We were just talking about taking you to the airport.

MONA: This is a mess. I'm sorry.

KAMAL: Ten different things, of course, suddenly happen.

MONA: We were just trying to put all this back. Here:

(*Directs* AZIZ *to a chair:*)

MONA: sit here. How are you feeling? I'm sorry you have to go back so soon after you've just gotten over your jet lag.

AZIZ: No matter. I like flying. It knocks me out, but I like it. I'm one of the few people who loves airplane food. I used to drive Hoda crazy asking her to lay out my food exactly like they do on planes. You know, so you discover your dessert in this corner, and your fruit-salad in that, and the bread and cheese here. It always made me feel like I was going somewhere. I think it was one of the many things that drove her to her death.

MONA: You mustn't say that. It's not true.

AZIZ: I know. But I like to think I had a hand in all the important events in her life. I think she would like me to think so too.

KAMAL: "Allah yarhamah." I'm sorry she is not here.

MONA: She always spoke of you with nothing but compliments and love. Very rare so late in a marriage.

KAMAL: Is Murad coming?

AZIZ: Still sleeping. He stayed up late, thinking. He no longer wants to become a doctor, you know. I can't say I understand his reasoning.

KAMAL: I am sorry to hear that.

AZIZ: What can one say?

(A bedroom door slams off-stage.)

MONA: Let me get you a cushion.

AZIZ: I am very comfortable, no need.

MONA: So you can put your leg up. Kamal? *(She points to the coffee table as she heads for exit.)* "Ana asaf giddaan." Our house is not usually like this of course.

(KAMAL drags the coffee table to where AZIZ is sitting.)

AZIZ: Don't trouble yourself.

KAMAL: We wanted to clean everything out for the—the...

AZIZ: I'm sorry you went to this much trouble.

KAMAL: No, no; we needed a big cleaning anyway.

MONA: It's healthier for the carpets. *(Small, awkward beat)* I'll get you a cushion. Excuse me. *(With one last look to KAMAL, she exits.)*

AZIZ: It's me who should apologize for spending all my time here in bed.

KAMAL: Now that you're well, why not stay a few more days?

AZIZ: You have been kind enough as it is.

KAMAL: Stay. We'll take you around. Show you some of the places you should see.

AZIZ: "Ma'lish." Another visit. The sooner we get back, the sooner Murad starts to think about what he wants to do.

(Slight beat)

KAMAL: Honestly, Aziz…perhaps it is best the engagement is off. For Murad's sake.

AZIZ: I don't think so. Huwaida would have been very good for him.

KAMAL: It's not Huwaida. Touch wood, out of all my children, she is the sanest. Until her decision anyway. It is this country. It will turn strange switches on and off in people's heads and make them act in ways you don't understand.

AZIZ: You mean Huwaida changing her mind?

KAMAL: For instance. If she was in Cairo, the better choices would be more obvious. She wouldn't have to wonder. Here, they are so desperate to sell you anything, they will make madness seem like a good choice if it can make a dollar.

AZIZ: This is everywhere.

KAMAL: Because this insane place is everywhere and the thinking that goes with it. It is frightening to think I don't have to miss an American T V show when I travel to Cairo because it will be playing there. No one around the world can get away from it.

AZIZ: You are right. Though I confess to being a big fan of *The Bold and The Beautiful*. *(Another popular T V show can be substituted.)*

KAMAL: Aziz, no; believe me. It is much better for Murad that this is off. You have no idea what disasters can fall on your head here. Here the sky will fall and the earth will open. The sky will fall on top of you, and cover the hole you have fallen through. That is how bad it can get.

AZIZ: What is it, Kamal? You speak as if something else is the matter.

KAMAL: No, I'm just saying. —I sometimes wonder why we came here.

AZIZ: But you have done well for yourself.

KAMAL: How? Money-wise? What does that matter if you lose everything else?

AZIZ: Why do you say that? Like what?

KAMAL: No—it's...never mind. I do not want to burden you with my problems.

AZIZ: Tell me.

KAMAL: *(Hesitates, then)* For instance...one of my sons.

AZIZ: What is it? May he be well.

KAMAL: Yesterday he decides God is a joke. Complete nonsense.

AZIZ: Who?

KAMAL: Tawfiq. Suddenly he informs me. My son has evicted God. Imagine.

AZIZ: Really?

KAMAL: Just like that.

AZIZ: And what was his reasoning?

KAMAL: He didn't say. He didn't leave it open to discussion. It was, in fact, like he was serving an eviction notice. No room for anything. God is no longer in his life.

AZIZ: This is very interesting. I would like to speak to him.

KAMAL: I would not inflict him on you. You are still recovering. Besides, he is too stubborn to have his mind changed just like that.

AZIZ: I would not try to change it. It is rare to meet a real atheist. I have met many godless men, men who say they believe in God but live lives that include everything but God. But an atheist? This is hard to find in Egypt.

KAMAL: This is what I mean. Yes, it can happen anywhere, but here you are encouraged. I swear, Aziz, we are ready to pack up our bags and follow you to Cairo.

(MONA *enters carrying a cushion.*)

MONA: And why would we do that?

AZIZ: I do not see how this is so terrible. If reasoning is what led him to this conclusion, then reasoning can lead him out.

MONA: Who are you talking about?

(MONA *puts the cushion on the coffee table.* AZIZ *will stretch out his leg on it.*)

AZIZ: "Shukran."

KAMAL: Tawfiq.

MONA: Kamal. We don't need to bother Aziz with Tawfiq.

AZIZ: What bother? This is intriguing. Every family should have an atheist. It keeps God's voice fresh and the faithful on their toes.

KAMAL: Aziz, please; you of all people. When it is happening to someone else's family it is intriguing, when it is yours, it is like an open wound with salt pouring in.

MONA: So why mention it? Can I get you something to eat? A lemonade?

KAMAL: I was telling him how lucky it is the engagement is off.

AZIZ: I am back on the fast, thank you.

MONA: *(To* KAMAL*)* And why would that be? I'm
sure we don't want Aziz to leave with the wrong
impression.

KAMAL: I was using our son as an example of how
this place can rob you in more ways than it can give.
And why Murad would be better off finding a wife in
Egypt.

MONA: I would not be so quick to use our children as
examples. *(To* AZIZ*)* And I'm sure such things have not
stopped happening to families in Egypt. Are you sure I
can't get you anything?

KAMAL: No, Aziz, go home and warn anyone who
thinks of coming here to appreciate what they have.
It's much better than anything they think this place can
offer. You have permission to use us as an example.

AZIZ: I always admired the courage you had in coming
here.

MONA: *(To* AZIZ*)* Do you think it is God-fearing of
someone to be blind to the gifts Allah gives us? And
keep moaning when all around you is evidence of the
good things you have?

KAMAL: You speak to me of blindness? You who ignore
your children's problems and not take responsibility?

MONA: *Me* be responsible?

KAMAL: *(Overlapping)* Excuse everything they do so
they grow up thinking one behavior is as good as
another.

MONA: And where were you, outside watching?

KAMAL: You make it so every time I speak to them
I have to scream because you are cutting the legs of
everything I say.

MONA: No, sorry, do not use me as an excuse for your
screaming, you enjoy it too much.

KAMAL: *(To* AZIZ*)* This is what I'm talking about.

MONA: There is nothing the matter with our family.

KAMAL: No, nothing at all, except we're losing our religion and our souls and to you that's a detail.

MONA: Maybe it's not God he's stopped believing in. Maybe it's you. Have you thought of that? Everything you stand for, and do to keep this family together when everything you do ends up strangling us a little bit more each day, making it so none of us can breathe.

AZIZ: My friends. My friends. Whatever is the problem, we will solve it. Please. It hurts me to hear you say these things.

(The front door slams shut. They all turn to the living room entrance. HUWAIDA *enters still dressed in her just-shy-of-being-gaudy outfit, with full make-up, red lipstick and all. In this company, the effect appears even more garish.* HUWAIDA *freezes.* KAMAL *and* MONA *stare at her.)*

HUWAIDA: *(To* AZIZ*)* Uncle….

AZIZ: Hello, my dear.

HUWAIDA: I…didn't know you were…

AZIZ: I had to come and say goodbye. And see your face. I haven't seen you all week.

HUWAIDA: Is—Murad here?

AZIZ: No. He's resting. Packing. You look…very beautiful.

HUWAIDA: *No.* No; this is. No: nobody was supposed to—. I didn't realize anybody would be here. This is not what I—this isn't what I usually wear.

AZIZ: It's okay if it is.

HUWAIDA: No it's not. This was for a school—thing. I feel like a complete idiot wearing this.

MONA: What are you doing?

HUWAIDA: Is Hamza home?

MONA: *What are you doing?*

HUWAIDA: Is he okay?

MONA: Answer me!

HUWAIDA: It was for a meeting with a professor. She was criticizing me for wearing the hijab and I wanted to show her how ridiculous the alternative was.

KAMAL: You succeeded. I hope she gives you an "A".

HUWAIDA: Nobody was supposed to see this.

MONA: Nobody where, on the street?

HUWAIDA: I just got so irritated with this teacher.

MONA: What were you thinking? Go in and change at once.

HUWAIDA: That's what I came home to do. Is Hamza—?

MONA: *(Interrupting)* Go in and change!

KAMAL: *(Referring to* HUWAIDA*)* Exhibit one.

*(*TAWFIQ *enters, stopping near the entrance. He's about to address his parents when he sees* AZIZ.*)*

TAWFIQ: Oh. Hi.

AZIZ: "Ahlan wasahlan." How are you?

TAWFIQ: I'm—good. *(To his mother)* Could you...

MONA: Thank you. Stay and talk with 'Am Aziz. *(To* HUWAIDA*)* And you, get out of that now. *(To* AZIZ*)* I'm sorry, I have to leave you for a moment.

*(*TAWFIQ *looks at* HUWAIDA's *outfit.)*

AZIZ: Is everything alright?

MONA: Yes. It's Hamza. He's not feeling well.

AZIZ: It is not serious I hope.

KAMAL: *(With some irony)* No. Not serious at all.

HUWAIDA: *(To her mother)* I'll come with you.

MONA: *Change.*

(MONA and HUWAIDA exit.)

KAMAL: *(To AZIZ)* You wanted to talk to him. Here he is. Exhibit two. And perhaps if exhibit three comes down, you will go home happy. Happy you live somewhere else.... Perhaps I will go bring him down myself. *(He looks off-stage, then exits.)*

AZIZ: "Masha'allah." Since I last saw you, how you've grown. And grown some more.

TAWFIQ: Between twelve and twenty—that's when it usually happens.

AZIZ: *(Motioning him over)* Quick.

(Or perhaps AZIZ goes up to TAWFIQ and takes him by the arm.)

AZIZ: Before something else happens and you are called away. Let us talk. I want to know all about it. Tell me everything.

TAWFIQ: About what?

AZIZ: For a few minutes, I would be delighted to get in your mind and see the world as you see it. That would be a gift to me.

TAWFIQ: What are you talking about?

AZIZ: Your father told me. About you and God.

TAWFIQ: Oh. That.

AZIZ: Is it true? Come, sit. Or stand if you prefer. Whatever you need to think clearly.

TAWFIQ: Is what true?

AZIZ: Are you an atheist?

TAWFIQ: *(Wary at this sudden interest; hesitating)* Er—
sure. I'm not a big one for labels, but I guess that's the
word.

AZIZ: Excellent. That is what I want to know about. Tell
me. Now that you don't believe in God: how does the
world appear to you?

TAWFIQ: How does...? —What, you mean—not
believing in God...do I see the world differently now?

AZIZ: Yes. Very good. Do you?

TAWFIQ: Um. Why? This is so hard to imagine? I'm not
exactly freak boy here. It's called waking up.

AZIZ: Excuse me for my excitement in wanting to
know, but I wish to know what *I* cannot imagine. It is
my failure, truly, and so my curiosity. I want to know
what you have woken up to.

TAWFIQ: I've—just woken up.

AZIZ: To what? You were in this cloud of believing,
yes? And then suddenly it clears, and you see what?

TAWFIQ: It's not like I'm seeing anything new. I've just
stopped wasting my time in believing in something I
don't see. And that frees me up to think about what I
do. *This* life and not some next that might, or might not
exist. And to care about that. Instead of all this God
talk which is like Santa Claus to me.

AZIZ: Good, good, continue.

TAWFIQ: That's it.

AZIZ: No. There must be more. What else?

TAWFIQ: That's just it. There's nothing complicated
about it. You just—wake up. And that's liberating. It
frees you up. I feel like I've been handed the deeds
to my own life and that I now own it for the rest of
my time here. I don't have to make like—mortgage
payments to some unseen whoever whose existence

has not been proven to me. Why hand your life over in that way? That's so crippling to me.

AZIZ: And so, what is it that gives you hope? Strength? It is God for others, for you?

TAWFIQ: Me. Relying on me.

AZIZ: Just you? A religion of one?

TAWFIQ: And each other. That's the point, relying on each other.

AZIZ: But then, if there's no God, some would say, why do anything? Why not do as you please? Be cruel when you want and kill when you feel like it.

TAWFIQ: People do that with God in their mouths all the time.

AZIZ: Yes, sure, these people speak his name, but in their hearts he is not there. They have collapsed into the worst parts of themselves. And that is us, not the religion. We fail the religion.

TAWFIQ: Which religion? They can't all be right.

AZIZ: Why not? Do we not speak different languages? One is not superior to the other.

TAWFIQ: That's just it, you may say that, but in your heart everyone goes around thinking their religion is just a little bit better than the next. And that little thought becomes the poison that ruins anything good about the religion.

AZIZ: But you can't judge God by the people who claim to speak on his behalf. We are not perfect enough to speak of something that is.

TAWFIQ: But then why speak of him at all? If God is a language no one can speak properly, then why bother? Why not just shut up about it. Just—once and for all—
shut up.

(Slight beat)

AZIZ: And yet people can not. —We can not seem to shut up about God. Anywhere. Is that not a puzzle in itself? —We chatter on about him like fools. Like the weak people we are. Going on about someone we can not finally prove. I can not prove anything to you about Him. The evidence I would show you that He exists would be the same evidence you would show me to prove that He doesn't exist. And your argument should win the day. It should, really. We don't hear His booming voice. He does not appear to us. He does not make State-of-the-World addresses like the president here. Maybe God is something that happened to people long ago because they didn't have television. Something to amuse themselves in the desert. And God is a pretty good story, so why not. And yet...people still do not let go. Why? We should have to come to the conclusion by now that He does not exist. But so many continue with this fairy tale not because as you say we are weak, but because—finally, we have to admit...we don't know. And perhaps as important as any faith—is the equal need to surrender to the fact that—we don't know. And can never know enough. And not all the hard facts and knowledge of science could ever satisfy the longing of wondering if this is all there is. And to live that with all the faith and passion we have. And if not believing gives you that same excitement, then, maybe, you and I can end up believing in the same thing. That we don't know enough to ever close our eyes to anything. Especially to the fact of us being alive, right now, here, talking, as witnesses to that. Whether you call that miracle biology. Or God. And maybe in that way, we both move forward as...believers.... Yes?

(Slight beat)

TAWFIQ: That seems like a stretch to me.

AZIZ: Well of course it's a stretch. I've traveled two continents and an ocean to get here. Traveling a few more feet to you shouldn't be that difficult.

(The doorbell rings.)

AZIZ: Come here and kiss me and show me you know how to end a good discussion. *(He takes a step towards him.)* I like you. *(He kisses him on the cheeks.)* You grew up just as I hoped you would. You grew up to surprise me. But be patient with your parents, they worry.

TAWFIQ: *(Referring to doorbell)* I'd better get that.

AZIZ: They want to know you're okay and not changing into something very strange.

TAWFIQ: I might.

AZIZ: Okay, but become strange in stages. Don't do it all at once and shock them too much.

(MONA enters.)

MONA: *(To TAWFIQ)* Aren't you getting that?

TAWFIQ: *(To AZIZ)* Excuse me.

(TAWFIQ exits to open the front door.)

MONA: *(To AZIZ)* Where's Kamal?

AZIZ: I don't know; he went through there. How is Hamza?

MONA: He's well. Thank you for asking.

AZIZ: Would you like Murad to take a look at him? I can tell him to come over?

(MURAD and TAWFIQ enter.)

AZIZ: You enter just when you are needed. Go and see what is the matter with Hamza.

MONA: Murad. "Ahlan." How lovely to see you. Come in.

MURAD: Hello, auntie.

MONA: *(She has gone up to him to kiss him on the cheeks.)* Now that you're both here, you'll stay for "iftar."

AZIZ: We do not want to trouble you.

MONA: What trouble. We prepared for an engagement. The least we can offer is dinner.

AZIZ: *(To* MURAD*)* Go and take a look at Hamza.

MONA: No, really, he is just tired from school work. He'll be fine. Now tell me you'll both stay for "iftar." We'll have all this put back in a second. *(Referring to the furniture)*

AZIZ: It is up to Murad.

*(*MURAD *is about to answer when* HUWAIDA *enters still dressed in her outfit. Some of the make-up has been removed, but enough remains. Perhaps she holds the cotton pad she was using to wipe it off. Slight beat)*

HUWAIDA: Hi.

MURAD: Hello.

(Slight beat)

MONA: *(To* MURAD*)* For your information, what she's wearing was for a school project: "The psychological effects of dressing badly to see if you can age your parents more quickly." It has worked. *(To* HUWAIDA*)* Please go back and come out properly.

HUWAIDA: *(Still looking at* MURAD*)* I will.

MONA: Do it now, please.

MURAD: Yes. Thank you for the invitation.

MONA: You'll stay for dinner then?

*(*MURAD *doesn't respond.* MURAD *and* HUWAIDA *continue to stare at each other.)*

AZIZ: *(To* MONA*)* Mona: on my way in, I noticed the lovely garden you have talked of many times. I saw plants I didn't recognize. Would you show them to me?

MONA: *(Sensing the need to exit)* Of course. —This is a good day to be outside. —Tawfiq?

TAWFIQ: What? ...Oh...sure.

MONA: *(As she leads AZIZ)* Then afterwards we will put all this back so we can eat properly. *(To HUWAIDA)* Okay? *(Then)* I really wish you would change.

(MONA and AZIZ exit. TAWFIQ lingers by the door, looking back at his sister and MURAD.)

HUWAIDA: *(To TAWFIQ, defiantly)* What?

TAWFIQ: *(Slight beat)* Whatever. *(He exits.)*

HUWAIDA: I always seem to be wearing something not quite right around you. Why is that?

MURAD: I have shown up when you don't expect me?

HUWAIDA: You have a bad habit of doing that.

MURAD: I would ask if you wanted me to leave again, but I am worried you would say yes.

HUWAIDA: *(Referring to her clothes)* If this doesn't scare you away.

MURAD: It was for a school project?

HUWAIDA: What if I told you it wasn't. —That this is how I wish to dress from now on. That I'd suddenly discovered a new me and she wanted to dress just like this.

MURAD: I would diplomatically suggest the new you should consult with the old you. And maybe a fashion consultant.

HUWAIDA: I'm serious. What if I decided I wanted to wear this from now on? And let's say, for argument's sake, we were married. What would you do?

MURAD: But you do not seem happy in it.

HUWAIDA: What if I decided I was.

MURAD: I would be...interested to know...how you came to this decision. And I would—start turning down the lights in the house. And become interested in shopping for women's clothes.

HUWAIDA: Never mind.

MURAD: Maybe this should be my new career. Helping women dress.

HUWAIDA: We can change the subject now. This was for an experiment, as a matter of fact. I am very inclined to experiments. And I reserve the right to make them. The expression "going out on a limb" is dear to me.

MURAD: I enjoy going out on a limb too. Perhaps it is the same limb that we are interested in.

(Slight beat)

HUWAIDA: Would you help me set up the table?

MURAD: Yes, of course.

(Over the next exchanges, HUWAIDA and MURAD assemble the table and place the chairs around it. Also, the remaining pieces of furniture are put in their place so that by the end of their scene, the living room/dining room looks orderly again.)

MURAD: Your art class went well? I hope I didn't make you miss too much.

HUWAIDA: No, I got there on time. We were drawing still-lives. Only the still-life was alive, and very nude. Which they didn't tell me beforehand. I think they thought they were going to have a laugh at my expense. Let's see how the hijab-wearing Muslim deals with a male nude. Ha, ha, aren't we cool. God, people can be so righteous. Using me to feel good about themselves. "Look how modern we are." No, you idiots, you're as stuck in your own crap as everyone else is. —Sorry. It just ticks me off.

MURAD: Most of my still lives are dead.

(*This stops* HUWAIDA *for a moment.*)

MURAD: Cadavers. For purposes of study.

HUWAIDA: Oh. Right. That can't have been fun.

MURAD: No, it was not.

HUWAIDA: Now *that* would freak me out. Alive and naked is one thing. Is that why you didn't want to become a doctor?

MURAD: A part of it. —Also, our teachers. The example they set. I found the more I learnt the less I remembered why I was doing this. I was getting further away from the reasons I wanted to become a doctor. I worried by the end I would care more about how much I would make than caring for patients.

HUWAIDA: But isn't that the case with most disciplines? For a while you get caught up in the details and forget the bigger picture. And don't you have to do that, sort of, if you want to get good.

MURAD: Perhaps. —I'm not sure I have explained it properly…. I felt it more important to protect the reasons for wanting to be a doctor, than to lose those reasons and become one. It sounds selfish, I know…. I just felt the way we were being taught was wrong.

HUWAIDA: Then maybe you should learn all that you have to, get some experience, then go back and teach it the way you think it should be taught.

MURAD: Yes. —That is also possible.

HUWAIDA: Being an idealist isn't bad. It's good. You just have to follow through, right? …I think you'd make a great doctor.

MURAD: *(Slight beat)* It is possible.

(Slight beat)

HUWAIDA: Let me take that.

(HUWAIDA *takes whatever piece of furniture* MURAD *was holding and puts it in its place.*)

HUWAIDA: There. Half-way livable again. It was driving us all nuts. Thank you.

MURAD: Not a problem.

(Slight beat)

HUWAIDA: Murad... Were you upset that I'd cancelled the engagement? Or secretly relieved?

(MURAD *looks at* HUWAIDA.)

HUWAIDA: I just felt... *(Then)* Perhaps you were also... *(Slight beat)* I'm glad you came though.

MURAD: Why?

HUWAIDA: I'm just glad you did. It was rude of me to suddenly change my mind like that.

MURAD: You have that right.

HUWAIDA: And you? —Did you come back to say goodbye? ...Or did you hope I'd change my mind?

MURAD: I came back to see if I had changed my mind.

HUWAIDA: Have you?

MURAD: No. I have not. *(Slight beat)* That, and also—I had a—a very strange dream.

HUWAIDA: Really? I've been having a few of those. What was yours about?

MURAD: Oh—it is...it is very complicated. —Perhaps I will tell you another time.

HUWAIDA: I'd like that. Dreams can be so weird, can't they? *(Slight beat)* I think I'll go change out of my experiment.

MURAD: It was a very interesting experiment.

HUWAIDA: More may follow.

MURAD: I do not doubt this.

(HUWAIDA and MURAD look at each other, smile.)

HUWAIDA: I won't be a moment. *(She turns to exit, at the door she turns back to him.)* Oh. By the way. Can I draw you sometime?

MURAD: With or without clothes?

HUWAIDA: I think your face will be naked enough for me.

MURAD: Good. Because I catch cold easily.

(HUWAIDA smiles. Exits. MURAD stands there for a moment before he turns to survey the room. He seems a little more pleased than when he first entered. Like something's been decided.)

(Then H D strides on carrying flowers. She is dressed as in his dream, wearing the hijab. She goes up to a vase and puts the flowers in. She turns to MURAD, who is watching her, flabbergasted. She smiles at him. He continues to stare at her. We hear AZIZ's voice.)

AZIZ: *(Off-stage)* It is amazing. This garden should be in a magazine. I don't believe Kamal did all this.

(At the sound of the voices, H D leaves through the kitchen exit.)

MONA: *(Off-stage)* This is where he goes when he can't talk to anybody. He plants something. Or digs.

(MONA and AZIZ enter. She carries a bunch of flowers.)

MONA: *(Sees the tidied room)* Ah, at last. Thank you. Did Huwaida make you do all this?

MURAD: (*Still digesting* H D's *appearance*) We did it together.

MONA: Murad, what she was wearing: please don't think she has lost her mind.

MURAD: I don't think she is the one losing her mind.

(MONA *has gone up to the vase to put her flowers in and sees the other flowers.*)

MONA: I didn't notice you had brought flowers. How beautiful. Thank you.

MURAD: I—don't—remember bringing them myself.

MONA: They are lovely.

(MONA *finds another vase for her flowers.* TAWFIQ *enters on his way to see* HAMZA. *To* TAWFIQ:)

MONA: Help me in the kitchen. I want to start bringing the plates and food out.

TAWFIQ: I wanted to check on—

MONA: He's fine. Help me inside. (*To* AZIZ *and* MURAD) Now that we have a living room, relax. We'll bring out the music player and listen to some music.

(MONA *takes* TAWFIQ *by the arm and leads him out.* AZIZ *goes up to* MURAD *and looks at him.*)

AZIZ: We are staying?

MURAD: I don't know.

AZIZ: You know. Your eyes say you know, and your heart is dancing like it already hears the wedding music.

MURAD: It's not up to me.

AZIZ: Yes it is. I saw her. She knows too.

MURAD: Ba-ba. We'll see. Let's just see.

AZIZ: We shall. "Inshallah."

(MONA *enters carrying a tablecloth, and behind her* TAWFIQ *carries plates and cutlery.* MURAD *goes up to help them.*)

MONA: Kamal's checking on the food. All the dishes to remind you of home. Or remind us, anyway.

(HUWAIDA *enters dressed in her hijab.*)

MONA: Now that's more like it. That way we can all digest our food.

HUWAIDA: That look happens to be in for some people.

MONA: Some fashions are worth ignoring. Now please go into the kitchen and get the napkins. Thank you.

(HUWAIDA *smiles at* MURAD, *then heads for the kitchen. She almost bumps into* KAMAL.)

HUWAIDA: *(To her father)* Hi. —We're laying out the table.

(KAMAL *doesn't answer,* HUWAIDA *exits.*)

AZIZ: *(To* KAMAL*)* A fantastic garden. I'm impressed. Where did you learn this? This is like a professional. You should have a side-business, landscaping. Carpets and landscaping. You take care of the inside and the outside.

KAMAL: *(Half paying attention)* Yes. Hello Murad. Welcome.

MURAD: Hello, uncle.

(MURAD *goes up to him and* KAMAL *kisses him on the cheeks.* KAMAL's *manner has changed: more somber, less energetic than we've seen him.*)

AZIZ: I am not flattering you. This is a skill. And the colors.

KAMAL: *(To* MURAD*)* It is good to see you.

MURAD: It's good to see you too.

KAMAL: *(To* MONA*)* Where is Hamza?

MONA: He is still resting.

KAMAL: Ask him to come down please.

MONA: It is better if he rests.

KAMAL: Ask him to come down.

MONA: Kamal, he's tired.

KAMAL: Are you embarrassed that he should be here?
—I will get him myself.

TAWFIQ: I'll get him.

(TAWFIQ *exits. Slight beat. There is a clear change of mood in the room.*)

KAMAL: *(To* AZIZ) I'm sorry. You came at a bad time.

AZIZ: Not at all. We are happy to be with you. It has been a long while since we have all sat down for "iftar" together.

(HUWAIDA *enters with a tray of glasses and napkins.* MURAD *goes up to help her.*)

KAMAL: Murad. Sit down. You shouldn't be helping.

MURAD: It's alright. I want to.

(HAMZA *enters followed by* TAWFIQ. HAMZA *stops near the doorway,* TAWFIQ *goes around him and helps with whatever remains to be done at the table.*)

TAWFIQ: He was—coming down anyway.

AZIZ: "Salaam 'alaykum," "ahlan beek," come here. I'm sorry to hear you're not well.

(HAMZA *goes over to* AZIZ. AZIZ *kisses him.*)

AZIZ: You and me. We must recover together and give each other strength. You are looking well, though. I don't see any fever.

MONA: He's taken on too much this semester. And with this changing weather.

KAMAL: That is not the reason.

MONA: Not the only reason, but it doesn't help.

KAMAL: It has nothing to do with that.

(Slight beat. Awkwardness)

MURAD: *(To* HAMZA*)* Hello.

HAMZA: "Salaam."

(Slight beat)

MONA: We can start putting out the food. It's a while yet, but why not start.

KAMAL: No. It can wait. If you don't mind. I'd rather we not do that now. Everyone, please; sit down. We still have time. Sit. Please sit.

(Perhaps KAMAL, HAMZA *and* MONA *remain standing.)*

KAMAL: Yesterday, Aziz…my son…was…he was practicing a song. He has taken up the oud, you know.

AZIZ: Wonderful, like his grandfather.

MONA: Kamal.

KAMAL: Let me finish.

AZIZ: "Gidak" would be very proud. This is the instrument he loved.

KAMAL: Yes, he did. And yes, he would be proud. I never could play it. —And sometimes the sounds my son makes tells me he too has trouble playing it. —But it doesn't matter…. When you're in love with something…the faults—the errors—what do they matter? They get you a little closer to what you want. And the sounds you know are there. And so—you keep going. —You find out all the music you shouldn't make—on your way to finding out the music you should…. It would be nice if Hamza would play for us what he has been practicing. —I would like that.

(HAMZA *stands there, not moving.* KAMAL *picks up the oud and walks over to him. Gently:)*

KAMAL: If you don't mind…. You said you were practicing, didn't you?

(HAMZA *nods.)*

KAMAL: Then that's all that matters.

(HAMZA *takes the oud.)*

AZIZ: You mustn't be shy. You're playing in front of friends and family.

TAWFIQ: That's usually the worst crowd to play for.

MONA: Tawfiq.

TAWFIQ: Well it is. Lots of "friendly" criticism.

HAMZA: It's still very rough.

KAMAL: It doesn't matter.

(KAMAL *goes to stand by* MONA. HAMZA *either sits or stands as he readies to play.)*

HAMZA: I'm not sure you'll like it.

KAMAL: We'd like to listen anyway. —You're my son…. Whatever you play will be just fine.

(Perhaps KAMAL *takes* MONA's *hand. Slight beat.)*

HAMZA: Alright… Alright.

(HAMZA *looks to his mother and father. Looks to his instrument. He takes a breath. Then:)*

(Light change. Everyone freezes. H D enters carrying a dish which she places on the table. She approaches the audience.)

H D: The thing I like most about Ramadan? …It's not the eating at the end of the day, which, let me tell you, can really hit the spot after a day of nothing passing your lips. And it's not the fasting itself, though yes, it encourages you to remember God. And yes, you can get a high after the first few days when your body

stops crying out for the basics and you begin to settle
down for the long haul. That's all good. But—what
really makes Ramadan special for me—is the time just
before we eat. When the whole family and the friends
you've invited gather around the table and there's this
wonderful anticipation of something delicious about to
happen. Of relief. And bounty. Of something about to
be shared. And it's that. That's the thing that makes the
month of fasting extra special. The sense in the room
that you've all been through something together. Most
times of the year you come to the table all in your own
little worlds, but at Ramadan—you come to the table
experiencing a shared world. And that simple thing, all
by itself is amazing. Oh, sure, the family dramas don't
stop. People can be just as petty and silly and quarrels
will happen because we are who we are, damn it. But
if you quiet down and pay attention, you may get a
glimpse of being a part of a bigger, and better drama
than your own. And that the people you're with are
the only ones who will help you play it out. In a way
that will make your part in it shine, along with all the
others. And that you're with these people. With them
in a way that sometimes escapes you the rest of the
year. —And so, you sit down. You pass the food. And
just before that first glass of water is drunk, all these
good feelings come to a head. So that the first thing
that passes your lips is tasted by something deeper
inside. And maybe, somewhere, God enjoys that as
much as we do. Maybe even applauds this struggle
we have taken on. And somewhere in our hearts …
perhaps we do too.

(Slight beat. Blackout)

END OF PLAY

Made in the USA
Middletown, DE
08 January 2025